Wicked
TACOMA

Wicked TACOMA

KARLA STOVER

THE
History
PRESS

Published by The History Press
Charleston, SC
www.historypress.com

First published 2021

Manufactured in the United States

ISBN 9781467148443

Library of Congress Control Number: 2021934321

To my husband, Ed, who helps me with the research, and my brother, Tom Wakefield, who died while this was being written. And to my parents, who loved history and loved to read and shared them both with me.

CONTENTS

CONTENTS

INTRODUCTION

First as a territory and then as a state, Washington was (and still is) unique among the lower forty-eight states, thanks to its bordering a foreign country on the north and being almost split in half by Puget Sound—a uniqueness that seemed to invite bootleggers, smugglers, gangsters and various other miscreants. The malefactors loved nothing more than a port town such as Tacoma with its hard-living loggers, railroad men, seafarers and miners. When an old-growth cedar was felled, people hollowed out the trunks, added a roof and lived in the stump. When

Typical cedar stump house, vintage photograph.

the outhouses were gamey enough, men hung their long johns inside because the accumulated odors killed the fleas and other vermin trapped in the fabric. Drunken brawls on Pacific Avenue, raids on brothels, opium dens and gambling establishments occurred regularly. Bootlegging and smuggling, often Chinese laborers but generally alcohol and narcotics—opium, morphine and cocaine—were common. Every time laws were passed to ban something, an informal (read illegal) sector sprang up to make it available. And while other waterfront towns began, early on, to clean themselves up, Tacoma kept its bad reputation until well beyond the 1950s.

RAILROAD TIMELINE

July 1, 1862: President Abraham Lincoln signs the Pacific Railway Act to provide federal government support for laying tracks for the first transcontinental railroad, funding to come by "authorizing the issuance of government bonds and the grants of land to railroad companies."

July 2, 1864: Congress charters the Northern Pacific Railway Company to connect the Great Lakes with Puget Sound. The railroad is granted "a potential 60 million acres of land in exchange for building rail transportation to an undeveloped territory."

1870: The Northern Pacific makes Jay Cooke and Company its exclusive bond agent.

1870: Brigadier General John W. Sprague becomes the railroad's Western Division general manager.

1870: Northern Pacific Railway scouts come to Cowlitz County to find a place for a terminus on the Columbia River and hope to file for a Donation Land Claim. The claim is a no-go, and the railroad ends up purchasing seven hundred acres in Kalama for its terminus and headquarters.

1873: Jay Cooke and Company overestimates its capital and advances too much money, which precipitates the Panic of 1873. While Congress attempts

Tough terrain. *Courtesy of the Library of Congress.*

One of the first engines on the Northern Pacific line. *Courtesy of the Library of Congress.*

to revoke the Northern Pacific's land grants, the army has to provide survey and construction crews to protect the laborers from attacking members of the Sioux, Cheyenne, Arapaho and Kiowa tribes.

1873: Backers of the railroad struggle to find financing.

July 4, 1873: Seattle's Arthur Denny reads aloud the following telegram: "We have located the terminus on Commencement Bay." Work begins immediately and has to be done before the end of 1873.

December 16, 1873: The first steam train arrives in New Tacoma.

THINGS DID NOT GO SMOOTHLY

Building railroads from nowhere to nowhere is not a legitimate business.
—Cornelius Vanderbilt, railroad magnate

The railroad's land grant depended on having the tracks laid to Tacoma by December 31, 1873. However, when Jay Cooke declared bankruptcy, the payroll dried up. Many of the down-on-their-luck prospectors who were laying the tracks felt that a "damned corporation" wasn't going to cheat them as geology had done and decided to walk off the job. A remaining skeleton crew carried on until the tracks reached Clover Creek, at which time they barricaded the grade and said they wouldn't work until they received their back wages. The men set up a camp and called it Skookkumville after Edward. S. "Skookum" Smith, the prime contractor. Skookum was described as "a handyman engineer from New York, who would try his hand at anything; sawmills, coal mining, steamships, politics, even building a railroad without cash." But with adequate provisions, the men were prepared to wait it out.

Trouble started in November 1873, when General Sprague and Sheriff D.W.C. Davisson approached the site and tried to remove some of the ties. They were ordered to stop and warned that removing more ties would be "at the peril of their lives." Davisson went into a tirade, but Sprague talked to the men and arranged a truce. The next day, Kalama, Washington clergyman W.T. Chapman went to the camp and preached to the workers. He was followed by three trains from Olympia bringing Governor Elisha P. Ferry;

Brigadier General John Sprague.
Courtesy of the Library of Congress.

Chief Justice Roger S. Greene; retired major Hazard Stevens, attorney for the railroad; J.C. Ainsworth, the Northern Pacific's West Coast manager; and General Sprague. It was 9:00 a.m.; they stayed until 5:00 p.m. Ainsworth did most of the talking and put up $500. The men agreed to accept it plus $5,000 "coming by way of the governor," brass and iron tokens good in trade at the Hanson Ackerson Mill and a free excursion over the line to all those who stayed and helped finish laying the tracks to Tacoma.

Skookum Smith was "a hard-driving man." During November, he pushed his crew to get the tracks laid into and through Lakewood, past Gravelly Lake and Steilacoom Lake, deciding "on a cheaper shortcut down a steep grade instead of…the longer route along Puget Sound." Then, it was on to New Tacoma, where, on December 15, residents heard the locomotive whistle. The last stake was driven in on December 16, 1873.

EVERYONE WANTS THE NAME "TACOMA"

December 25, 1864: Job Carr canoes from Gig Harbor looking for a place to homestead. He chooses a site on Commencement Bay and calls it Eureka.

April 1, 1868: Morton Matthew McCarver arrives at Commencement Bay because, at that time, a site somewhere on Puget Sound is considered to be the railroad's likely terminus due to its proximity to Snoqualmie Pass.

November 30, 1869: Anthony Carr, Job's son, files a town site plat on land he owns and calls it Tacoma. McCarver purchases land from Job Carr and plats a town site to be called Commencement City. Philip Ritz, a railroad surveyor, persuades him to name the site after the mountain. "Tacoma" is taken, so McCarver's site becomes Tacoma City.

July 14, 1873: Seattle resident Arthur Denny reads aloud to a gathering of Seattle citizens a telegram that announces that the railroad terminus will be on Commencement Bay.

February 3, 1875: The railroad decides to have the terminus in a town of its own. The site chosen is slightly southeast of Tacoma City. The railroad calls it New Tacoma.

Looking down on Old Tacoma. *Courtesy of the Library of Congress.*

November 28, 1883: The legislature passes "An Act to Consolidate the Cities of Tacoma and New Tacoma, under the Name of Tacoma," to become effective on or after the first Monday of January 1884.

BEFORE WASHINGTON
WAS A TERRITORY

Charles Wren, the First Bad Boy

*D*riving from Tacoma to Roy, just off 8th Avenue South on JBLM property, is the little Wren family grave. It has three markers. The one on the left reads "infant"; the one in the middle is for Elizabeth Ross Wren, who was thirty when she died on January 5, 1851, of dysentery; and to her right is a marker for her husband, Charles D. Wren, who died on February 24, 1873. Looking at the lonely grave site, which is on an overgrown knoll in the middle of a vast prairie, it's easy to grieve for the young mother and child, but Charles Wren was a community irritant until the day he was forced out of town.

Wren was a Canadian citizen, a mixture of Cree Indian, Scotch, Irish and English, born in 1827. He came from Red River Valley, an area that would eventually be shared by Canada and the United States, and he was one of the first settlers in what would become Pierce County. Wren started out as an employee of the Hudson's Bay Company, an unhappy experience from the company's point of view. "A drunken ne'er-do-well," said the company factor, Dr. William F. Tolmie; "the most desperate character I ever knew," said neighbor Charles McDaniel. Others added to their descriptions, saying Wren was a ruffian and bully who lived and thrived in the eye of the hurricane.

On November 15, 1848, almost two years before the Donation Land Act became a law, Wren filed a claim for 641.62 acres of land on Muck Creek (then called Douglas Creek). Never mind that the land belonged to the Puget

⟶WASHINGTON TERRITORY VIEWS.⟵

A territorial view, circa 1885. *Courtesy of the Library of Congress.*

Sound Agricultural Company. However, his claim was eventually signed—the second land claim in the county signed by President Ulysses S. Grant.

Almost immediately, Wren set about becoming a wealthy man. According to Charles Prosch in his *Reminiscences of Washington Territory*, Wren's cattle had "the most remarkable breeding qualities." In spring, while his neighbor's cattle produced no calves, each of Wren's cows seemed to give birth to two or three. And within just a few years, his herd was the largest in the area. When cattle buyers came along, he was the only rancher with animals to sell.

In his *Journal of Occurrences at Muck Station Puget Sound Agricultural Company*, Edward Huggins wrote, "Two inches of snow on the ground this morning.... The cart went to the Fort [Nisqually] for beef. Found a lot of our best mares were in Wren's barn, drove them away, Wren not at home."

Historian William P. Bonney, secretary of the Washington State Historical Society, wrote that Wren "figures in court proceedings perhaps more than any early settler…both civil and criminal."

Wren's first appearance was on February 8, 1849. He was a plaintiff in the court of the county's first justice of the peace, Judge Thomas M. Chambers. Wren said that two men, John and Walter Ross (Ross was his wife's maiden name, and among her siblings were brothers John and Walter, but no relationship claim was made in court), had broken into his home, assaulted him and threatened his life. Sympathy was not on Wren's side; it was assumed the men were "victims of Wren's branding iron."

After Elizabeth died, Wren married her sister, Mary Amelia. Both women were of Ojibway/Metis/French ancestry. "Metis" ancestry means "a person whose lineage is a mixture of indigenous and Euro-American heritage." During the Puget Sound Indian Wars of 1855–56, Wren, along with other former Hudson's Bay Company men who had married Natives, was suspected of aiding the Indians. Nineteen men, Wren included, were ordered held at Steilacoom. When he tried to return home, Wren was forced back. Governor Isaac Stevens wrote that Wren's "conduct had been especially bad."

In 1868, the *Washington Standard* reported an assassination attempt on Wren as he sat one evening in Olympia's Pacific Hotel. Not long after that, two of his neighbors, Charles McDaniel and Andrew Burge, waylaid him a few miles outside Steilacoom, tied him to a tree and commenced whipping him, after which they warned him to leave town. They left him "suffering in his ropes." Burge was known to be a hothead, and Wren and McDaniel often directed their criminal activities at each other.

According to Puyallup mover-and-shaker Ezra Meeker, gambler and thief McDaniel was as bad as Wren. Once, when McDaniel was brought to court for hitting someone over the head with a gun, the jury was afraid to bring in a conviction. Hearing the verdict for acquittal, Justice Samuel McCaw shouted to the panel of men, "By God, that verdict's all wrong. I'll set it aside and fine you and send you to jail." It wasn't something the law allowed him to do, but Sheriff Stephen Judson was ready to carry out a sentence, so McDaniel paid a hefty fine.

Not long after the trial, a Black man moved into the area and spent most of his time out on the prairie hunting and fishing. One day when Burge happened to be driving home, he was shot in the neck. The Black man disappeared, and it was later learned that Wren had hired him to kill both Burge and McDaniel—undoubtedly, one of Pierce County's first murders-for-hire. By the time the information came out, Wren had left the area. Hearing that, McDaniel, a man named Gibson and several others jumped his claim. A mob of thirty or forty "law-abiding" citizens then decided the claim jumpers needed to be punished. They attacked them in a narrow passage between Gravelly and Steilacoom Lakes. Gibson was wounded and loaded into a wagon; McDaniel took off toward Steilacoom. At the edge of town, Gibson managed to get off a few shots from his wagon bed and wound two men. Someone then shot him through the head. Reaching Steilacoom,

McDaniel hid in a saloon. When the mob approached, he left his gun inside and went out armed only with a knife. He said he wanted to be heard. Since Gibson had spilled the beans, someone in the crowd shouted, "Shoot him," and they did. McDaniel ran, was hit and collapsed. According to Meeker, he was left writhing on the ground until he died two hours later.

Sheriff Isaac Carson, who had been locked up at the time, arrested seventeen alleged vigilante members; all seventeen were found innocent.

McDaniel's grave is near Western State Hospital; his marker reads, "Chas M. McDaniel Born in Iowa 1834 and died at the Hands of Violence Jan 22, 1870 Aged 36."

Andrew Burge is probably the octogenarian described as "one of the road builders for the government near Tacoma" who was alive and living in Yakima in 1910 when he accidentally drank a liniment containing belladonna, chloroform and aconite—"enough poison to kill a hundred men." A doctor saved him, and Burge lived five more years, dying on March 23, 1915.

Charles Wren moved to Canada and worked as a butcher, but he died in Tacoma on February 24, 1873.

Part I

A NEW TERRITORY

Chapter 1

THE BATTLE TO BAN
CIGARETTES

*W*hen Washington became a territory, it created a seal with an immigrant wagon and a log cabin backed by a fir forest on one side and, on the other side, the Goddess of Hope pointing "to a sheet of water with a sailing vessel, a steamer, and a city in perspective." Included is the word *Alki*. The Native American word translates to "by and by" or "hope for the future." That "hope" included banning cigarettes, whiskey and wild, wild women.

March 1893

Report of Conference Committee House Bill No 236:

Mr. Speaker, we your committee to whom was referred House Bill 236 "An act making it unlawful for any person or persons to buy, sell or give away or manufacture cigarettes or cigarette paper and providing the punishment for the violation thereof " have had the same under consideration, and we respectfully report the same back that recommendation hereto.

Respectfully submitted, C.T. Claypool.
Chairman Senate Committee: C.T. Roscoe
Chairman House Committee:
Trusten P. Dyer,
C.L. Webb
J.T. Eshelman,
L.C. Gibman

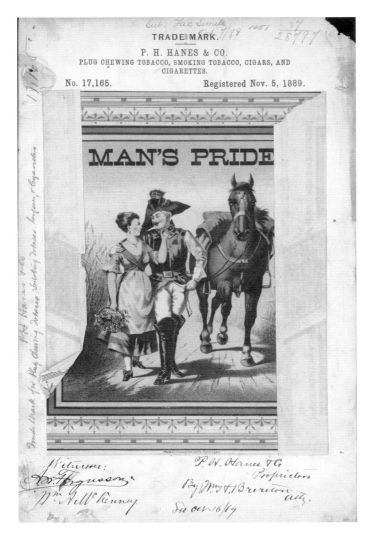

P.H. Hanes and Co. for Man's Pride brand plug chewing tobacco, smoking tobacco, cigars and cigarettes. *Courtesy of the Library of Congress.*

Though tobacco had been a legal, not to mentionable a lucrative, crop since the colonial days, in the 1880s and 1890s there was a move to ban cigarettes for moral as well as health reasons. Smoking cigarettes was seen as a highly addictive habit that "would entice youths to try more dangerous substances such as alcohol or drugs." Temperance advocates equated tobacco with the evils of saloons and pushed to have "coffin nails" outlawed.

Attempts to enact a federal cigarette prohibition failed, even though members of Congress "acknowledged that smoking was a public health hazard." Instead, they suggested that it "be dealt with at the state level."

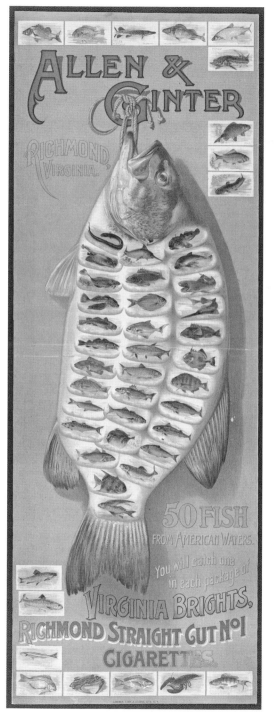

Fifty fish from American waters.
You will catch one in each package
of Virginia Brights, Richmond
Straight Cut No. 1 cigarettes.
Courtesy of the Library of Congress.

Making cigarettes was a cottage industry. *Courtesy of the Library of Congress.*

Washington State's movement came ten years after the Woman's Christian Temperance Union (WCTU) established a Department for the Overthrow of the Tobacco Habit. In 1893, C.T. Roscoe, an Everett Republican, introduced House Bill 236, which would make it illegal for people to "buy, sell, give away or manufacture cigarettes or cigarette papers." Violators could spend six months in jail or pay a fine of up to $500 ($14,715.39 in 2021). Both chambers passed it, though the Senate also wanted to make possession illegal. However, on March 7, 1893, when Governor John H. McGraw signed the bill, it did not include the "possession" amendment. Washington's passage kick-started other states into enacting their own anti-smoking laws: North Dakota in 1895, Iowa in 1896, Tennessee in 1897 and Oklahoma in 1901 until, by 1901, eleven different states had some kind of anti-smoking law. Unfortunately, claiming the law "interfered with interstate commerce," a legal challenge popped up.

In July 1893, the U.S. District Court in Seattle ruled against the state, a decision the *New York Times* hailed as "defending the rights of consenting adults to engage in a habit that was recognized as objectionable." The legislature repealed the law in 1895 and "rejected a couple of attempts to reinstate it."

Eight years later, cigar-smoking senator Orville A. Tucker sponsored a new ban but only on cigarettes. It failed. However, the legislature did manage to pass another prohibition in 1907. This one made making, selling, trading or giving away either cigarettes or cigarette paper illegal. To get around the court decision, wholesalers involved in interstate commerce were exempt. Two years after that, possession of cigarettes and rolling paper was also banned.

SOME THOUGHTS ABOUT BOY BANDITS

If home is not pleasant, there are streets. The boy who is driven there for his company finds it. He also finds cigarettes and whiskey and profanity. He finds the society that makes Jesse James a saint and Deadwood Dick a martyr.

—*Tacoma Times*, March 26, 1904

Things came to a head when William "Big Bill" Haywood, organizer of the Industrial Workers of the World, more commonly known as the Wobblies, made a speaking tour of the state. He was first arrested in Ellensburg for rolling his own cigarettes, but "the Kittitas County prosecutor declined to prosecute because he felt the law was unconstitutional." Next, Big Bill was arrested in North Yakima and fined $9.50 plus court costs.

In his autobiography, Haywood himself credited his convictions for the law's eventual repeal, which finally happened in 1911.

Chapter 2

LIQUOR, TERRITORIAL LEGISLATION AND THE LOCAL OPTION

No sooner had Washington become a territory than George Whitworth, a Presbyterian missionary from Indiana, organized the territory's first temperance society, pushing for total abstinence. The question of the sale and manufacture of liquor was taken up by Washington's territorial legislature in its second session. Total abstinence failed by eighty-six votes. Washington seemed to be in a reform mood, though. Laws were passed "requiring businesses to close on Sunday"; making it a misdemeanor if a woman appeared in public wearing men's clothes, unless on the way to or from a masquerade party; and curbing gambling.

Throughout the 1880s, as women in Washington gained (and lost) the right to vote, they continued to push for prohibition. The year 1886 saw the territorial legislature pass the "local option," giving towns the right to vote on the issue "within their own community." The law was repealed and then modified to allow pharmacies to sell liquor. The modified version stayed on the books until 1909.

When Washington's constitution was created in 1889, convention delegates "had an opportunity to include state-wide prohibition in the document, along with women's suffrage, and where the state's capital would be located." The men rejected prohibition and women's suffrage.

When an anti-saloon league went into action, events outside the state were conspiring against it. Those who wanted to ship meat and produce long distances began experimenting with steel instead of wooden railroad cars, as well as with insulation, ventilation, forced air, ice, ice bunker bulkheads,

Anything for popularity. Cover of *Puck* magazine. *Courtesy of the Library of Congress.*

vertically adjustable grates and perforated floor racks. In 1880, the United States Patent Office issued the country's first patent for a mechanically refrigerated railroad car. Twelve years later, the Bottle Seal Company developed a cap called the crown cork bottle stopper. The cap allowed bottles to be stored upright. The combination of the two meant liquor, or the products needed to make liquor, could be shipped nationwide.

In 1909, the local option was voted back in. However, members of the Anti-Saloon League weren't about to give up. Temperance supporters flocked to the "dry" towns to patronize businesses there and show their approval.

On November 3, 1914, local voters approved an initiative outlawing the manufacture and sale of liquor, though, if you could get it, you could drink it. Beginning on January 1, 1915, the law allowed "people with permits to import up to two quarts of hard liquor or 12 quarts of beer every twenty days." But with a prescription, one could purchase spirits at a drugstore. One Monday, a tongue-in-cheek *Tacoma Times* reporter wrote that "drugstores must have closed early on Sunday because only 16 drunks appeared in police court."

Once again, though, actions outside the state went into play. According to Historylink.org, "On March 3, 1917, the United States Congress approved the so-called Bone-Dry Amendment to the 1917 Post Office Appropriations Act. This amendment forbade shipment of intoxicating liquors of any

Old Crow Whisky label. *Courtesy of the Library of Congress.*

kind into states which had bone-dry laws, whether or not those states had permit systems." And then, four weeks later, the country entered World War I. A new Food and Fuel Control Act, aka the Lever Act or Lever Food Act, went into effect. It gave the president the right "to limit or prohibit the use of agricultural products in the production of alcoholic beverages." The legislation was unpopular, especially with wheat farmers, and quietly disappeared in 1918.

However, by 1920 the Volstead Act was in effect, so state and city legislation no longer mattered.

Various items seized were held until 1941, when federal officers in Tacoma "carried out a court order" to destroy "confiscated liquor and assorted bootlegging paraphernalia, some dating to 1928." A local reporter wrote that previously held in a vault in the federal building were "jugs of mash, unadulterated moonshine, moonshine in bottles with fancy labels and with phony labels, Canadian whiskey, Scotch whiskey, empty bottles and packages of phony labels, flavoring material, coloring material and corks." As "R.W. Crowell and Louis Kindt, officers in the alcohol unit, poured the alcohol down the sink, a wag walked by and said, 'Let me have a drink of that just for old time's sake.'"

Chapter 3

POLITICAL SHENANIGANS

Not Exactly Bad Boys, But...

On February 22, 1889, as one of his final pieces of legislation while in office, President Grover Cleveland signed the enabling act, authorizing the election of delegates to conventions in Washington, Montana and the two Dakotas. The purpose of the conventions was for men to draft constitutions in the four territories and present them to the people for approval, thus allowing for statehood.

Seventy-five constitution makers met in Olympia throughout the summer of 1889, and on August 22, they presented a draft to voters. All but two of the articles—prohibition and women's suffrage—were approved. Next, a penmanship expert was contacted to write up the necessary documents for presentation to the president. And last, a special pen for the president's use in signing the documents was made from gold panned in the state. When the scroll was ready for the secretary of the territory to affix the seal, he attached it lightly so as not to mar the beauty of the manuscript.

In late October, Olympia resident J.W. Robinson took the forms to Washington, D.C. Formalities were observed, and Robinson was taken to President-elect Benjamin Harrison's office. Unfortunately, when the president opened the scroll, the seal fell off.

"I won't sign this," he said. "The certificate has come off."

"But, Mr. President," said Robinson, "it's just come loose. It was attached." However, the president refused to sign, and Robinson had to wire officials in Olympia and ask them to send another copy with the territorial seal firmly glued on. Ten days later, Robinson took the new scroll to the president and, with a flourish, also presented the gold pen for his use.

"This steel pen I always use is good enough for me," the president said and signed Washington into statehood ten days late, on November 11, 1889.

In the meantime, a number of men had been campaigning for the positions of the state's first senators. Two of them were Tacoma banker Walter J. Thompson and Northern Pacific Railroad man Brigadier General John W. Sprague. At election time, Sprague was losing but refused to drop out. In the end, Pierce County's vote was split, and both men lost. Bad luck for Tacoma.

About the same time, a congressional committee had been touring Puget Sound with an eye toward establishing a navy yard. Neither John B. Allen from Walla Walla nor Seattle's Watson C. Squire, the two senators-elect, had any interest in promoting Tacoma. The navy ended up expanding an existing facility at Mare Island, California. Not until 1903 was the Thirteenth Naval District formally established in Bremerton.

As if this weren't enough, Tacoma also missed becoming the state capital.

In 1905, Pierce County legislator George Stevenson, known in politics as the "Big Bludgeon," was busy courting the railroads. Olympia officials were counting on railroad expansion to help develop the state and make communication more convenient. Unfortunately, Thurston County senator A.S. Ruth wasn't cooperating. So to punish Ruth, Stevenson introduced a bill to change the location of the state capital from Olympia to Tacoma. The idea started as a bluff, but the bill easily passed the Senate and went on to the House.

In a panic, Ruth began to muster up Thurston County friends, including Representative John O'Brien Scobey, to push for defeat. However, to everyone's amazement, the bill also passed the House. Friends of Tacoma, who pointed out that the governor, Albert E. Meade, had been nominated in Tacoma, thought the move was most likely a done deal. The chamber of commerce sent a delegation of judges and local businessmen to Olympia to offer Wright Park as the site for a new capitol. Never mind the fact that the heirs of the Wright estate threatened to sue for recovery of the land if it was used for anything other than a park. Around the state, our motto, "Watch Tacoma Grow," became "Watch Tacoma Crow." In the end, however, it all came to naught. John Scobey paid Meade an unexpected visit and persuaded him not to sign the bill. The governor had promised an Oregon newspaper the opportunity to break the story. To get the scoop first, a Seattle newspaperman called the governor and told him he knew of the veto. It was a trap, and Meade fell into it. He forgot his promise and gave the Seattle reporter full details. In doing so, the governor wasn't very popular in Oregon, and for quite a while, he sure wasn't popular in Tacoma.

Cascade Mts., Puget Sound, and the Pacific Northwest.

707. On the trail to Paradise Valley, Mt. Tacoma or Rainier, Wash. 6

Copyright, 1906, by J. A. Blosser.

On the trail to Paradise Valley, circa 1906, Mount Tacoma or Rainier, Washington. *Courtesy of the Library of Congress.*

About the time the Northern Pacific Railroad arrived, Tacoma was ready to live up to its catchphrase: the City of Destiny. The Indian War was over; men and women had climbed Mount Rainier for the first time; and a woman, Janet Steele, owned an Old Town hotel in her own name. But even earlier (in 1873), with Edward Smith donating land, the Hanson and Ackerson Mill providing the timber and George Atkinson providing the motivation, down in Old Tacoma men built St. Peter's Episcopal.

True, Tacoma was going through a "pig period," with the animals trotting up and down the streets and stealing from grocery stores, and there was an earthquake, but then a literary society formed and the first telephone was installed.

589. OLDEST CHURCH TOWER IN AMERICA. TACOMA WASH.

Views of the Cascade Mountains, Puget Sound, and the Pacific Northwest.

The oldest church tower in America, in Tacoma, Washington, 1906. *Courtesy of the Library of Congress.*

The railroad accommodated the comings and goings of a variety of people, but long before the Chinese were forced out of town, 126 citizens signed a petition "suggesting" sewing machine salesman C.E. Spencer leave. His crime was to have called the recently deceased president, James Garfield, "a knave, a rascal, a scrub and a swindler."

Charles Wright was welcome, but Henry Villard wasn't.

January 1878 was so warm that men mowed their lawns and sold the grass.

Tacoma, Seattle and Portland were regularly competing with or criticizing one another.

And Tacoma was rife with crime.

Chapter 4

POPULATION 1,008

Shanghaied? As Many as Possible

Take my advice, my lad, [he said]…*and enter the service cheerfully.*
—*from the memories of Robert Hayes (1789–1847), victim of a press gang*

Whether the stories are true or not, history-wise, there was probably not a Puget Sound port that didn't have problems with shanghaiing. Forcing a man on board a ship against his will was a common occurrence. During its formative years when Aberdeen was known as the "Hell Hole of the Pacific," one of its best-known residents, Billy Gohl, was believed not only to have shanghaied dozens of sailors but to have killed many more.

In the nineteenth century, sailors had no rights, and shanghaiing filled a captain's need when he couldn't find a crew. If necessary, captains often looked to a "crimp," frequently the owner of a boardinghouse used by single men. To entice sailors into their hostels, crimps had minions labeled "runners" meet and board ships in the harbor and woo the men. Once at the rooming house and with their belongings stored away, the hapless marks were "plied" with cheap liquor sometimes spiked with opium. When they passed out, and since the boardinghouses were often built on pilings over the water, it was easy to drop an unconscious man through a trapdoor to a rowboat that took him to awaiting ships.

On the United States' Pacific coast, Portland eventually surpassed San Francisco in the custom, but when it came to shanghaiing, Tacoma was no stranger to the practice.

Down on the dock, loading a sailing ship, circa 1907. *Courtesy of the Library of Congress.*

On March 4, 1891, Captain McWhinnie of the ship *Sierra Cordena* made light of the fact that while on the way to Tacoma, he'd lost one of his men. In talking to a reporter for the *Tacoma Daily News*, he said, "We had variable weather, with some gales and some calms. There was one thing I think of, now you have spoken. I will have to report it. I lost one man overboard a few days out of Montevideo. He fell from a yard [arm] on the mainmast."

However, a young Swedish sailor on the same ship told a different story. "I was in Montevideo sick at the time the *Sierra Cordena* was lying in the harbor, there," Olaf Anderson said. "It was pretty hard work to get sailors to man ships from that port at the best, but some [of] the men in the harbor who might have gone on some of the ships did not wish to go on this ship. I was shanghaied on board the Bessel [*sic*] and have never

Looking toward the loading docks. *Courtesy of the Library of Congress.*

signed any papers nor in any way made a contract with the captain or his owners except verbally." He went on to say that he didn't know how he was put on the ship, that he'd told the captain that he'd been sick and had been shanghaied from the hospital and wanted to be put back on shore because he felt so bad, the result of recent surgery. He even showed the captain the scars. But the captain told Anderson he was all right and that he'd be paid for every day he worked and that he could leave the ship when they arrived at San Francisco. Once they were out to sea, he tried to get Anderson to sign papers, but the sailor said he refused because doing so would commit him to continuing on to England. "If it [his signature] is on any of the ship's papers," Anderson said, "someone else wrote it there, for I never did."

Anderson wasn't allowed to go ashore in San Francisco, nor would Captain McWhinnie pay him, saying the voyage would not be over until they reached Tacoma. Then, in Tacoma, McWhinnie tried to prevent his leaving the ship. Anderson left anyway, saying he would sue for salary due. Eleven days later, the ship was still in harbor while being loaded with wheat headed to the United Kingdom. Six months after that, Anderson was in court but suing the captain of another ship, the steamer *Quickstep*, for pay due from him, and the *Sierra Cordena*/McWhinnie affair seems to have disappeared.

While Anderson was suing, a sailor named August Peterson was having his own problems. He was on board the ship *Osborn* when Seattle men William (or possibly Thomas; newspaper articles differ) Garretson and James Turk attempted to castrate him. Peterson was taken to Fannie Paddock Hospital (renamed Tacoma General Hospital) for treatment. On December 3, he was down on McCarver Street in Old Tacoma when a gang of men grabbed him and tried to drag him to where the *Osborn* was being loaded with wheat before heading to Liverpool. Peterson put up what fight he could, and while the men were slipping a noose over his neck, he was able to shout for help. A police officer and two railroad men heard the shouts and rushed to his rescue. Peterson said that he'd initially agreed to sail with the *Osborn* but changed his mind when he learned that new clothing for the voyage wouldn't be provided. After his rescue, Peterson was seen in town until midday, but not after that.

On December 12, 1891, sailors instigated "a suit by libel" against the ship *Karoo*, complaining of being shanghaied and, while aboard, of cruel treatment and short rations. They said they were fed a mixture of sea biscuits and meat cooked in the "skimmings" of salt pork, a food they called "akouse" (probably lobscouse, a sailor's stew made from meat, vegetables and hardtack). The judge allowed the issue to proceed without advanced fees because the sailors swore they had no money.

The case went to trial on February 15, 1892, with the ship's captain claiming the sailors had fallen into the hands of shyster lawyers who ought to know better and, as a result, had become "emboldened to have fallen in the habit [of suing]." Various captains met on the wharf and held a conference in which they said,

LEFT TO ROT IN THE SUN

A serious reflection on the authorities of King and Pierce counties is the fact that for more than a week the body of a man cast up by the waves had been allowed to lie rotting in the sun on the banks of Brown's point opposite Tacoma.

—San Francisco Chronicle,
February 13, 1890

Loading lumber, circa 1906. *Courtesy of the Library of Congress.*

"Seamen shouldn't be encouraged to desert—that all having the shipping interests at heart," the complaints should be ignored.

At the trial, the judge said that as there was "no British counsul [*sic*] in Tacoma with whom to confer; that two of the lieutenants involved were American citizens so the case could not be taken out of the country; and that all of the libellants except two were brought to this country without having been lawfully bound by any contract," they were free to leave the ship and sue for wages. (In 1872, the United States passed the Shipping Commissioners Act. It said that sailors had to sign onto a ship in the presence of a federal shipping commissioner and that seamen had to be paid off in person. The reason for the act was to put paid to problems with crimps.) In conclusion, the judge said that since some of the men were foreigners and since the

Likely to Be Shanghaied.

Likely to be shanghaied. Old cartoon. *Author's collection.*

commissioner refused to sign them, and that at Rio de Janeiro most of the original crew had deserted, the *Karoo* must have been brought to Tacoma by a crew of whom none had signed shipping articles, as they were deserters from other ships. He also said that the men probably exaggerated the issue of starvation.

During the proceedings, it was proved that the captain hired a boarding master to provide a crew and that at least three of the men had been shanghaied. The captain then charged the shipping commissioner with negligence.

At the end of the trial, the judge found in favor of the seamen, with the Seattle *Daily Intelligencer* saying, "The decision rendered by Judge Hanford in the case of the claims of sailors of the ship *Karoo* for wages is commendable for its boldness, as well as for its manifest justice, from the court's point of view, after hearing and weighing the testimony."

Three months later, the same newspaper reported that Barney Hogan, an employee of the Tacoma Mill Company, had disappeared and was believed to have been shanghaied. And on May 21, the *Intelligencer* announced a $250 reward for the return of Puyallup Indian Peter Stanup, also believed to have been shanghaied.

On May 27, 1895, R. Flack, a former sailor and, at the time, an employee of Wheeler Osgood, disappeared, leaving behind wages he hadn't yet collected and all his personal belongings.

Seattle papers covered more stories about shanghaiing than did Tacoma papers, but the *Tacoma Daily News* did follow happenings in November 1897 when a man named Alexander De Flaron reported having been assaulted and beaten up. He swore out a warrant for the arrest of Dave Evans and James O'Ryan, two Old Tacoma boardinghouse men. De Flaron said he had signed on to the *Dashing Wave* as part of the coastal trade and that he'd gone to Evans's house to get his belongings. Evans wouldn't relinquish them, and O'Ryan demanded that De Flaron sign on to the ship *Glenark*, at port in Seattle. When the sailor refused, attempts using "verbal persuasion" gave way to "more vigorous arguments." O'Ryan hit him, De Flaron said, blacking both his eyes, and then stuck a gun in his face, while Evans used a shoe to pound on the seat of De Flaron's pants. That's what got him the most, De Flaron said as he swore out a warrant. He didn't care so much about the beating, but he hated to be kicked in the rear.

Seattle papers regularly covered reports of men being shanghaied and accused Tacoma of having more than its share of crimps, using large type if the incident took place here.

Chapter 5

A DIFFERENT KIND
OF BIRD CAGE

One day in 1884, a nice-looking woman dressed in business attire arrived in Tacoma. For a while, she shopped around, making small purchases and letting people know she planned to open an establishment offering flowers and singing birds for sale. Local residents, yearning for East Coast culture, enthusiastically made the woman welcome.

A week or so later, approximately five hundred businessmen received perfumed notes decorated with scrollwork announcing the opening of the Bird Shop. It was near Ninth and Pacific at the back half of the second floor of the building where Justice of the Peace Alexander Campbell held court. The sixty-three-year-old justice was pleased to be sharing his floor because, he said, "I love flowers and birds." He wasn't, however, very observant and didn't notice the sounds of music and laughter coming from his neighbor's quarters or see the lights burning long into the night. He didn't want to investigate but eventually had to. Yes, it was discovered, there was a bird cage—a gilded one—but the "birds" were actually the negligees the residents wore, and the flowers were "painted lilies" (the women).

The judge immediately drafted a letter to the city council asking that his court be relocated "away from the contaminating influences of The Bird Shop." Councilmen W.P. Bonney and Joseph V. Chamberlain, members of the city's Health and Police Committee, passed a resolution rebuking the police department for allowing such houses to exist and Justice Campbell for allowing it to exist in the same building as a police court and for his willingness to relocate, writing:

THE WHORE'S LAST SHIFT.

The whore's last shift. *Courtesy of the Library of Congress.*

It would be in the highest degree improper and against good morals and sound policy for this Council to declare by its action that within the city limits of Tacoma a house of ill-fame could necessitate the removal of a police court, and there is sufficient discredit to the city government, in the inefficiency of its police department without giving its official sanction to allow a house of ill-fame to more conveniently flourish.

Following this, one would assume the Bird Cage would have been closed down. *Au contraire.* The justice was allowed to relocate his court, and the Bird Shop was allowed to remain open.

Chapter 6

BAD ANIMALS OR
BAD ANIMAL OWNERS?

Domestic Pets

On January 17, 1896, two peanut vendors with stands near the Gross Brothers' Store at Ninth and Broadway got in a fight, and one of the men threw his merchandise, pieces of his cart, a steamer and various "show cases" at his rival. By the time the police showed up, the ground was covered with debris, candy and peanuts. Not to worry—all kinds of animals had always roamed Tacoma's streets, one being a pig known as Graham's hyena. From Tacoma's earliest days, various animals had free run of town, occasionally sleeping on or under the sidewalks. However, Graham's pig was only interested in food. One day, when a sack of flour was left unguarded in front of Nolan and King's grocery, the pig pounced and carried it away. Mr. Graham should have done what the owner of "a drove of hogs did": take his animals down to the waterfront to forage for food. A *Tacoma Daily News* reporter wrote that the swine "thrust their snouts into the sand and rooted up the clams.…All the time they are doing so crows are alighted on the backs of the hogs and proceed to swoop down on the clams as fast as they are exposed and fly up into the air with them, and dropping them to break the shells."

As far back as 1886, Tacoma had a city pound for "stray cows and horses, which had, in ages past, been wont to disport on sidewalks and in front yards at their sweet pleasure." The facility was completed on a Saturday, and on Sunday morning, seven head of cattle stood staring through their bars. The owners of five of the cows paid the fines and took the animals home, but the remaining two weren't alone for long; on Monday morning, "vigilant officers" brought in five horses and more cows. Those cows not claimed by their owners, who also had to pay for their keep, were auctioned off after five days.

Cleverly pointing out that there was no charge for entrance, the *Tacoma Daily Ledger* said within three days the city pound had pretty much paid for itself.

A pound for stray cows in Tacoma was all well and good, but it didn't help South Tacoma, where a police officer named O'Boyle spent a fair amount of time rounding up geese and ducks as well as chasing stray bovines. However, on August 5, 1904, he had to corral—as it were—three strays. Seeing what the officer was doing, their herder, Freddie Ludwig, tried to rescue his charges. To do so, he enlisted the help of a dozen playmates who "swooped down on O'Boyle," all the time yelling and creating so much noise that the cows scattered. Ludwig was arrested; no word as to the fate of the cows.

At that time, the "pound ordinance" had not been enforced south of Sixty-Fourth Street, but when residents of Fern Hill, Manito and Wapato complained to the mayor and city council, the pound law was extended. All cows had to be tethered.

Roaming cattle continued to be a problem, and in 1910, police chief Maloney told his men to be on the lookout for them as complaints were pouring in: residents of the Larchmont neighborhood wanted a "herd district." They were tired, they said, of having to protect their gardens from invading animals. Rumors spread that the Tacoma Railway and Power Company were behind the push for the "herd district." However, while the owners protested, keeping the animals contained was important because they regularly cavorted in Tacoma's drinking water.

According to the Humane Society's website, one summer day in 1888, "a drunken logger brought a bear cub to the corner of 8th and Pacific, where he began kicking it to get the animal to perform tricks. A crowd soon gathered and tried to stop the abuse, but the man refused. A Justice of the Peace was summoned, and the logger was arrested. Later that week, a group of town leaders met to form the Tacoma Humane Society—only the fourth such organization in the nation."

An October 16, 1886 newspaper article describes the city pound, located near Freeman and Young's stables, as "an agreeable innovation in Tacoma." The facility was eighty by eighty feet with a roof over half of it. At the time, Tacoma had five stables, and there is no information as to the location of Freeman and Young.

Horses were often as problematic as cows. In June 1897, Carl Mettler, a Swiss dairy farmer, was prosecuted for peppering horses with shot because they had broken down his fences, providing a way into his fields for stray horses and cows. The *Daily News* said, as "there are a number of farmers on the jury…it was unlikely Mettler would be treated badly."

Stray chickens could be as much of a problem as cows and horses. One day in 1885, during a children's program at East Congregational Church, a hen from a nearby chicken yard flew into the church and lit on the organ. When ushers tried to remove her, her flapping wings upset several vases of flowers, releasing water that flowed onto the organ, putting it out of commission.

A lawsuit between John Soakup and Dora Munslow in November 1907 brought in fans of both gardens and chickens. Soakup's yard was full of carefully cultivated roses. The rich, loamy soil attracted Munslow's chickens, which were afflicted with wanderlust. One day while they scratched around the newly planted bushes, Soakup threw a rock, hitting a hen and breaking its leg. The rest flew home; Munslow killed and ate the injured bird and then had the gardener arrested. At the trial, when a testifying patrolman said he had told Munslow to keep her birds in an enclosed yard, the case was dismissed. Munslow may have loved her chickens, but certainly not more than Jens Jensen, who slept with his.

Jensen was an aged Dane who, while living near Forty-Eighth and Alaska Streets, took up residence in his coop with four dozen feathered friends. There he cooked all his meals and slept on an old lounge under the roosts, using burlap bags and an old carpet as blankets. Health officials said he seemed perfectly happy with his living accommodations, and he rebelled at their interference. Judge J.M. Arntson said Jensen was "more to be pitied than despised or censured" and fined him fifty dollars, the fine to be suspended if the old man started work on new living quarters within seven days and tore down the old coop.

Another chicken-related case took place when C.A. Cavender petitioned the city to have roosters crowing between 1:00 a.m. and 5:00 a.m. declared nuisances. In response, city commissioners said, "If roosters want to crow, let 'em crow." Good news for Tige, mascot of the South Tacoma Tigers, an amateur baseball team.

Tige was a black-breasted, red game rooster belonging to ballplayer Johnny Bassey. Bassey was out of town when his rooster arrived, so Tige's home became a small box under the Olympic Cigar Store's counter. The Olympic was a vaudeville house at 902–08 Commerce Street, run by George

The Sad Story of Unlicensed Pets. 1890s newspaper sketch. Possession of Author

The sad story of unlicensed pets, nineteenth-century cartoon. *Author's collection.*

Shreeder. One April morning, employee Charley Bascom opened the theater and fed Tige, after which the rooster decided to take a little stroll down Commerce. Charley, who may not have been the brightest bulb, panicked and "turned in a riot call." Soon, clerks, waiters, waitresses and pedestrians swarmed the street, converged on Tige and closed in. The rooster was said to have given Charlie a dirty look as the crowd herded him back to his room.

Of all the roaming and/or stray animals, dogs seemed to cause the most controversy. As far back as 1890, dog owners had to license their pets, and not everyone was happy to do so. The cost of a license was one dollar for a male dog and two dollars for a female. By 9:00 a.m. one August morning in 1890, 153 licenses had been sold—mostly to women who brought their animals in to "have the clerk inspect their pet's good points and note their peculiarities and tell the dog catcher all about them so that he might not by any mistake endeavor to rob them of its companionship." Only one woman objected to the license fees, saying "she wouldn't pay $2 for her sweet Nellie when that nasty Fido of the Grimes got off for $1."

Certainly, stray dogs roaming the streets were a problem, and a dog catcher patrolled the streets daily, lassoing animals and bringing them in. However, there were complaints of the animals being tortured at the pound, and in 1893, a *Tacoma Daily News* reporter investigated. At the time, the facility was located in an area at Twenty-First and N Streets, and though noisy, it was found to be clean and well ventilated. The dogs appeared to be well fed, and males and females were kept separate. It was true that curs were quickly dispatched, but good dogs were kept and, if not claimed, were sold. As to execution, the dogs were put in a body clamp and shot in the head. Their corpses then went to what was called the chemical works and rendered down. The fat was shipped back east and made into soap. A report from the pound dated March 5, 1910, said 472 dogs had been shot.

Still, the stray dog problem persisted. In August 1909, some people living on the west side of town began poisoning them. In 1917, residents living on McKinley hill did the same; one victim was a fox terrier belonging to the British vice consul, C.E. Agassiz.

In 1928, the Wm. S. Van Voris Home for Friendless Animals opened at 2817 South Proctor Street; in 1937, the Humane Society housed animals in a shelter near Oakland. Finally, in 1951, the society received authorization to operate the city's animal control facilities.

Chapter 7

WILD ANIMALS AND SOME NOT-SO-NICE PEOPLE

Tacoma's handling of wild animals was all over the place. June 1894 saw Pastor Robbins of the Lincoln Park Baptist Church inviting all canary owners to bring their birds to a special celebration of spring. Their cages were suspended from the gas brackets, and when the organist began to play, he was accompanied by forty-nine singing birds. Frank Alling's "Oriental pheasants and quail," however, didn't fare as well.

In April 1897, E.S. Wheeler, general manager of the Dodwell, Carill & Company's Hong Kong branch, notified Alling that, per his order, "a fine crop" of the pheasants was coming on the steamer *Victoria* in the custody of the ship's captain. Alling planned to release the birds on his Fox Island game preserve. Eager to take possession, when the boat docked, Alling was one of the first persons to board it. Unfortunately, the hold contained no birds. When asked, the captain said he'd made Purser Gault responsible; Gault, in turn, said he'd instructed the Chinese steward to "keep a watchful eye on the birds." Among the ship's stores had been a quantity of quail on ice intended for the officers' mess. Misunderstanding his instructions, the steward had Alling's birds killed, cooked and served.

Not to be deterred, Alling ordered more birds and the following year received and released two dozen "Oriental" pheasant. Two special game wardens were appointed to guard the birds, and no hunting of them was allowed until they were well established.

Postcard of Chinese pheasants. *Author's collection.*

Alling's birds may have been protected, but not so grouse, prairie chickens, sage hens, native pheasant, ducks, plovers or even swans and sand hill cranes that flocked to the county, bringing joy to local hunters. George Klehlmeyer was the game warden in the 1890s, and the night before opening day of bird season, he generally headed south to the prairies around midnight to keep an eye on things. He often sent word to town that there were large flocks of both mountain quail and valley quail and even a few of Alling's "Mongolian quail." He also said that most people were respectful of the game laws, though duck hunters were very unhappy that the season closed on the first of January.

However, when it came to animals, large mammals had it rough. An undated article from the *Tacoma Daily Ledger* provides a good example. Tiny was a bear cub purchased by Messrs. Hardin and Rogers after its mother had been shot by Jack Charley, a member of the Puyallup tribe, because the pair had been seen near the reservation. The two purchasers then turned her (according to the papers, the cub was female) over to a trainer, and occasionally, she would box with members of the railroad crew. But Tiny wanted to be free. One day, she was unusually quiet, even refusing her candy treats. Then, suddenly, she grabbed the six-inch chain that kept her tethered to a post, "snapped it like a thread," climbed over a fence and took off for freedom. Hardin was summoned, and though he panicked, he started off in hot pursuit. A frightened boy told him he'd seen the bear headed for Knoell's Blacksmith Shop, but none of the men working there said they'd seen her. One of the workers joined the chase, and the bear posse cut across some vacant lots toward the Northern Iron Works, where Andrew Moe, a particular friend of Tiny's, worked. About that time, a wild cry came from the blacksmith shop, followed by silence. Anticipating the worst, Hardin became almost sick. Approaching the shop,

Hundreds of antlers of the elk are shipped to England from the Grays Harbor county [sic] every year. There are at least a thousand of the animals killed every year in Washington territory and Oregon hundreds of which grace the ancestral halls of England as ornaments.

—*Tacoma Daily Ledger*, undated

he saw Tiny fly through a window and hightail it off, taking the entire sash with her. The smithy workers joined the chase, following the bear down the hill, through the ironworks shop and across the Tacoma Flour Mill's engine room. Employee George Watson heard the shouts and glanced over his shoulder in time to see Tiny; he leaped over a fly wheel, "dodged behind the steam dome and went out a back widow to the ground by way of the smoke stack."

Tiny never stopped. She made a final leap and took shelter under the Tacoma Eastern Dock. Hardin offered a fifty-dollar reward, but nothing and no one could entice her out and back to her cage.

It was June 1891 when a hungry bear and two cubs were seen wandering near a pasture just outside town. When the cows who grazed there failed to return home, their owners, Mrs. Thomas Parkerson and Mrs. Elbridge Ackley, went to see why. The mother bear appeared to be old and weak, but she rose up and advanced toward them, waving her front legs and growling. Not about to lose their cows, each woman grabbed a piece of wood off a nearby log pile and advanced, waving it around. After a few tense moments, the female bear and one cub headed for a nearby copse of old-growth timber. Initially, the remaining cub was too weak to follow but eventually was able to join his family while the cows were rounded up. Had the women been armed, they could have killed the female, as there was a good market for bear skins—a market of which a local man named Jasper Woolery took advantage.

By 1895, Woolery had the distinction of having killed more bears than any other man in Pierce County. "Yes, I killed 34 bear during one spring," he told a local reporter. "I recollect the county was, at that time, paying a bounty of $5…and I made a rather profitable deal of it." By 1895, however, he was selling the hides for from $10 to $40 each. "I think the price has grown larger because of the extermination of buffalo, as bear skins are now used for robes," he said. At the time, he figured his total kill was up to 125.

Over in the Fern Hill neighborhood, one kill was enough for Joseph Jandos. Woolery may have been attempting to decimate the local bear population single-handedly, but in 1898, one adventurous bruin that dared to take on Jandos came out the loser.

The entire length of the Sperry Ocean Dock and the Puget Sound Flouring Mill. *Courtesy of the Library of Congress.*

Young Jandos was out bird hunting when he spotted black fur in the bushes and heard the ominous growl. Though his weapon was a shotgun and his cartridges were only loaded with fine birdshot, he decided to kill the bear. Birdshot filled the animal's nose but only served to make the bear angry. It started toward Jandos, who pulled out a knife and charged. One cuff of a hairy arm sent the man flying across a large log. Man and beast rose to their feet; the bear's teeth caught Jandos's left arm, bit deep and tore the flesh. Jandos, in turn, plunged his knife into the bear at a spot close to its heart. The animal rolled under a log, and Jandos, his clothes covered in both of their blood and hanging in tatters, went home to get some buckshot. He returned, found the bear and poured the shot into the animal's right ear. Then he fetched his father, and the two took the animal to town and sold it to a butcher. A local physician dressed the hunter's wounds, but he's not on the census taken two years later.

Though by 1920 Tacoma had become a trade center for furs, the first big sale was in 1906, with bundles of skins arriving from as far away as

White fox pelts, circa 1912. *Courtesy of the Library of Congress.*

Northern Siberia and delivered to West Coast Grocery for an auction. They included large numbers of bear; polar bear; mink; marten; otter; silver, red and white fox; a few sable; and some Bjelky skins. Wikipedia says the Bjelky is a type of dog from Siberia; the paper said it was an animal resembling a squirrel. Either way, large bundles arrived. The company's largest sale to date had totaled $63,000; the wholesale value of these skins was $30,000. Of only passing interest to the buying public were the whalebone and ivory included in the shipment.

The volume of business done by West Coast Grocery in 1919 was the company's largest. According to A.A. Pentecost, secretary and buyer, interest wasn't fading. "We have enough quotations on 1920 to convince me that prices in many instances will be higher than last year."

The Washington Department of Fish and Wildlife has state trapping regulations posted. But it's probably easier to pick up roadkill.

EIGHT BIRDS PITTED IN A PACIFIC AVENUE JOINT FOR $300 A SIDE

A number of sports gathered in a well-known resort on Pacific Avenue on Saturday night to Witness a cocking main. The birds were pitted by Hank Halstead and a man named Stone of Yakima. Each man put four birds in the pit. Three were taken out dead. The stakes were $300 and fell to Halstead.

—*Tacoma Daily News,*
January 2, 1893

Chapter 8

WHAT REALLY HAPPENED
TO PETER STANUP?

*I*t was May 19, 1893, when the *Seattle Daily Intelligencer* received word that the body of Puyallup Indian Peter Stanup had been found floating in the Puyallup River near the Tacoma tide flats. It was just nine months after he'd met with United States secretary of the interior John Noble to discuss the future of the Puyallup Reservation.

Most Tacoma locals have heard of Billie Franks Jr., a member of the Nisqually tribe, because of the addition of his name to the Nisqually National Wildlife Refuge. Stanup isn't so well remembered.

He was born in 1857 or 1858 probably on the Puyallup Reservation, where missionaries taught him to read, write and "cipher." Between 1880 and 1881, he attended Oregon's Forest Grove Indian School. Shortly after leaving there, he began writing to Pacific University's Professor Joseph W. Marsh expressing his wish to enter Tualatin Academy in autumn 1881 as a regular high school student. Pacific University had been established at Forest Grove with the support of the Presbyterians and Congregationalists. The academy was a college preparatory high school attached to the university. Stanup knew some of the professors, and the academy agreed to his admittance, but eye problems prevented his attendance. Nevertheless, the twenty-four-year-old studied and learned enough theology so that the Presbyterian Church licensed him in the summer of 1883.

Back home on the reservation, he became an interpreter, especially for the Presbyterian clergyman Reverend M.G. Mann. He also worked as a newspaper printer in Tacoma. "When a boy," Stanup said, "I made up

View of the Puyallup River and Reservation, circa 1897. *Courtesy of the Library of Congress.*

my mind to follow the printing business, and seeing an advertisement in an eastern paper headed, 'Every man his own printer,' and offering for $6 a rule, font type, and a press stick [a stick resembling a broom handle with one long, flat side that could be laid on a surface and pressed without its touching the rest of the paper], I made up my mind to become a printer at once."

Stanup saved his money and sent away for the kit. When it arrived, he visited the *Daily Tribune* office in Old Tacoma and learned to set type. "I printed cards for all the boys," he said.

He then went to Olympia and apprenticed himself to Frances H. Cook, who was publishing a small evening paper called the *Echo*. Three months later, the tedium of the job and a threat of tuberculosis caused Stanup to quit. He did, however, help move the office to New Tacoma.

Returning to the reservation, he spent several years preaching to his people. According to Myron Eells in his article, "Peter C. Stanup, Indians of Puget Sound," "His example and the prominence which he had obtained served as a spur to many of the younger generation," and it is said, "the general enlightenment that at present exists among the Puyallups is largely traceable to his influence."

Stanup was naturally bright and self-reliant. Though not a chief or of chieftain ancestry, he became an acknowledged tribal leader in the tribal relations with both the whites and the government. He was a good businessman, amassing a fortune valued at $50,000 (approximately $1,250,000 in today's currency), and for some ten or twelve years, he not only engaged in many land speculation enterprises for himself but also helped negotiate land deals between Indians and whites. Among the Puyallups, however, he is probably most remembered for going up against the Washington establishment, protesting the Dawes Allotment Act (DAA).

President Grover Cleveland signed the DAA into law on February 8, 1887. At its core was dividing tribal reservations into plots of land for individual households, with the following goals in mind: break up tribes

Photograph of a Puyallup couple, circa 1900. *Author's collection.*

Thou Shalt Not Steal, Thou Shalt Not Covet… *Author's collection.*

as a social unit; encourage individual initiatives; further the progress of Native farmers; reduce the cost of administrations to the Natives; secure parts of the reservation; and open the remainder to be sold for a profit to white settlers. As to the allotments, each family would receive 160 acres; each single person eighteen or older, 80 acres; those under eighteen, 40 acres. The secretary of the interior would issue rules to ensure equal distribution of water. Those eligible had four years to select their acreage, after which the secretary of the interior would do it for them; the federal government would hold the allotments in trust for twenty-five years. Natives receiving allotments were expected to live "separate and apart" from their tribe before they would be granted citizenship. The policies were supposedly put in place to protect the individual Indians against swindlers.

On February 13, 1892, Puyallup Indians met and discussed many things pertinent to the reservation, but the one issue on which they were nearly unanimous was their "desire to have Congress remove the restrictions" that prevented their ability to sell their land.

"About forty of the original 166 holders of patents [land] are dead," Stanup said. "And they died without money enough to buy the necessaries of life. Many others are dying in the same way. They, therefore, want to raise some money by selling part of their land. They cannot eat land, nor wear it."

Six months after the meeting, on August 22, 1892, Stanup waited on the reservation to meet United States secretary of the interior John Noble. Noble was coming to Tacoma on department business, gathering information from both the Puyallups and non-Natives. The Tacoma city leaders and entrepreneurs who greeted him as he got off his train wanted the sales and lease restrictions removed. That would give them access to the land and its resources. The Puyallups, they said, had left the land "woefully undeveloped."

From Tacoma, Noble traveled to the reservation for his meeting with Stanup and the reservation agent, Edwin Eells. Eells also opposed opening the land to development but only because he felt the "aboriginals still had a lot to learn about surviving in the white peoples' world." However, in mid-afternoon when Noble arrived, Stanup and a local reporter were the only men present to receive him. Eells wasn't there, and no explanation for his absence was ever given. Noble met with approximately two hundred tribal members and praised their command of the English language, the homes they'd built and how well they cultivated the land. His recommendation, he said, would be to permit the allottees to sell small portions of their acreage, but he would advise the authorities to collect the proceeds of the sales, hold the money in a trust and dole it out to the Natives in "measured portions." His reasoning was that "even white men are apt to lose their money, and if the Indians should lose theirs they would be sorry and blame someone, perhaps, for not helping them take care of it." The government, he said, "wanted, eventually, to give the Puyallups independent control of their various allotments but only after they'd shown they'd integrated into American society."

In the end, nothing came of the meeting.

Events on the night Stanup was believed to have died are inconsistent. One person said the Indian had eaten nothing but did have a small glass of liquor. Another claimed he'd seen Stanup in Tacoma; Lieutenant W.P. Goodwin said he'd gone to Stanup's tent to tell him about a fight he'd had with Edwin Eells. Stanup's wife, Annie, said he'd returned home but didn't come inside.

She said she'd heard him talking to someone, and then he left. That would tally with a neighbor's saying that the night of the disappearance, his dogs barked so furiously he had to get out of bed and lock them up. Also, boats manned by known shanghaiers had been seen in the bay. The only thing giving credence to that theory was the discovery of boot or shoe prints made by larger footwear than those the victim wore that led to a spot on the edge of the bay where a boat had been tied up.

Stanup's body was found in the Puyallup River on May 22, 1893.

The following day, a coroner's jury was summoned to hear the grim results of the autopsy report. On Stanup's left arm midway between the shoulder and elbow was a red spot consistent with a thumbprint. There were blood clots in both chambers of the heart, the pulmonary arteries, the vena cava and the veins. The aorta was empty. His lungs, stomach, kidneys and intestines were all normal. His head had been separated from his first vertebra in a way that suggested a violent twist.

Though on a personal level Stanup was well liked, not all of his business practices sat well, particularly with Agent Eells, who had been instrumental in securing a change of route for the Northern Pacific Railroad that took it through the reservation. The night before Stanup's death, Captain Gilbert S. Carpenter led G Company, Fourteenth Infantry, in an attack on the Indians guarding their land. The troops made a bayonet charge, and Stanup had the Puyallups roll logs on them from the hill above. Nor did Stanup's religious practices or political persuasion (he was a Republican) always sit well with other tribal members. Nevertheless, both the Puyallups and members of the coroner's jury believed he'd been murdered.

Funeral services for Peter Stanup were held on May 25, 1893, in a Catholic church, in keeping with his father's religion, and he was buried at the reservation cemetery. Two months later, a package containing his personal papers was found in the bay. They hadn't been in the water long.

The Indian Citizenship Act, which Congress passed on June 2, 1924, "granted citizenship to all Native Americans born in the U.S." However, "the right to vote was governed by state law; until 1957, some states [still] barred Native Americans from voting."

With the passage of the Indian Reorganization Act, "sometimes called the Indian New Deal, on June 18, 1934, federal legislation began the process of reversing the previous legislation." And by that time, Stanup was long since dead.

No one was ever brought to trial for his death.

Part II

··

GROWING PAINS

Chapter 9

NOTORIOUS

Peter Sandberg

Slavery still exists but now it applies only to women and its name is prostitution.
—Victor Hugo (1802–1885)

When the Northern Pacific Railroad finally arrived in Tacoma, the population was 113 white men, 12 white women and, interestingly, 2.5 Chinese. There were few mentions in the papers of ladies of the night, but with all the loggers and seafaring men, there was a need, and prostitutes set up shop on D Street, Railroad Street and South Thirteenth and C (Broadway). Newcomers to the city could find their locations in the Sporting Club House Directory.

On June 3, 1896, several "houses" were raided, resulting in 226 people signing a petition requesting "the removal of disorderly houses from D Street." The mayor, Angelo Fawcett, responded, saying, "I respectfully beg to inform you that I have decided, so far as possible, to prevent the spread of loose and immoral persons and women of prostitution to all parts of the city, and on account of the former city council not having set aside any prescribed section for these people to inhabit, and as the block bounded by D Street, Opera Alley [changed to Court C in 1905], Eleventh Street and Thirteenth Streets is and has been inhabited for a number of years by these people, that hereafter and until the council instructs otherwise they will be allowed to remain in said block." And so, an official red-light district run by gambler Harry Morgan developed. But starting in 1889, when Peter Sandberg arrived in town and set up shop on Thirteenth and A Streets, Morgan's red-light district got some major competition.

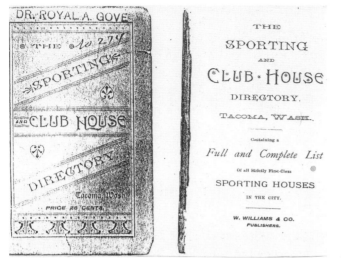

Tacoma's Sporting
Club House Directory.
Author's collection.

Sandberg was born in 1866 in the Swedish county of Troskefors bruk and at age twenty-three showed up in Tacoma. Initially, he worked for the Northern Pacific as a carpenter. Some of his contemporaries said that one day he went to a saloon for a drink, and the bartender spilled it all over the counter. Seeing the waste, Sandberg said the man would make a better blacksmith than a barkeep. The angry bartender tore off his apron and challenged Sandberg to do better—which he did—and before the end of the day, he had also bought a saloon.

Over the following years, Sandberg also bought several hotels, more saloons, gambling houses and a wholesale liquor business. However, he is most remembered for gambling and prostitution.

According to a *Tacoma Daily Ledger* reporter, the mayor's statement, "accomplished with much blare of trumpets, [was seen] to have been merely a sop thrown to the church-going people to whom he had promised much in the way of reform: a sop thrown in the apparent expectation of blinding the people to real conditions." The reporter went on to describe the continuing noise of decrepit pianos, ribald songs, the occasional violin or horn and the coarse laughter of men, boys and fallen women at five different dives: the Elk, 1546 C Street; the Marconi, 1520 C Street; the Rainier, 1512 C Street; the Almy, 1502 C Street; and the Old Pal, 1356 C Street.

The Old Pal's main attraction seemed to be a real orchestra and a woman wearing a loose red wrapper. The Almy, with Joe Carbonne as proprietor, had a side door known as the "Family Entrance" that led to a room lined with box-like private apartments popular with boys and some policemen. Frank

Petta ran the Rainier; his women were described as being of "ponderous fatness." The women who generally operated out of the Elk "had faces, neither of which was her fortune," and the Marconi, besides the usual, had a short lunch counter where men and women sat on stools to eat. One of the working girls said, "We get a commission of 40% on all straight drinks we sell. On sales like a quart bottle of beer we get half of 50 cents. I know one girl who made a $28.15 commission one Sunday night after 11 o'clock." She went on to say, "I have one room upstairs here and another down town. O [*sic*] yes, the police know us all; they have the names and addresses of all of us and know where we live. This is a pretty good place to work but in some of the places along here they allow colored men to mix with the white women and I won't stand for that."

In early April 1904, reporters from the *Tacoma Times* did some investigative reporting on a few of the more notorious dives. They started with the Owl Saloon, a gambling den described as "a poorly ventilated room about 16 square feet with air so foul it was stifling." The stench came from the sawdust floor. The room was entered from a barroom, probably one of Sandberg's, as the following month he was making repairs and alterations on the premises without a permit. At the west end of the barroom, two entrances led to the Phoenix, "a variety theater, where burlesque performances of the lowest class are held nightly." Scantily clad female "rustlers" sold liquor—and other things. Somewhere in the warren of places was the Globe Hotel, with a rear entry to a game room known as the White Elephant.

Saturday night. *Author's collection.*

From the labyrinth of Sandberg's place, the reporters hit the gambling and barroom known as the Board of Trade at 1328 Pacific Avenue. Five games were going on in the crowded room.

Next came the Warwick Saloon at 1205 Pacific Avenue, later referred to as "a den of iniquity." Harry Morgan owned it before he relocated to Opera Alley.

The night the reporters visited the Olympic Club at 902–08 Commerce Street, "well-dressed men sat behind stacks of chips in a small room in the rear of the bar." The previous day, three "touts" were arrested there, no reason given in the paper. At the time, the city had an ordinance against gambling taking place on an establishment's first floor. George Shreeder, the Olympic's proprietor, had gotten around it by building a platform three feet high and moving the roulette wheel and poker tables there.

The last place the newspapermen visited was the Senate saloon at 738 Pacific Avenue, about which they had little to say.

Meanwhile, the West Coast Wagon Company was doing business between A Street and Court A on Fourteenth Street. In August 1904, the company's management filed an application for an injunction for the suppression of Sandberg's "vile resorts." The injunction had three specific complaints. "Until lately," the owners said, "the[ir] company had numbered among its customers many ladies, who came to the factory for carriage repair work and to purchase articles manufactured by the company, but since the opening of [Sandberg's] Lincoln House, there [sic] have been prevented from patronizing the company." Next, they claimed, their company had lost value. "At the present time [our] business has a value of about $15,000, and but for Sandberg's resorts, the business would be worth $30,000, exclusive of the building, machinery and stock." And finally, they complained about Sandberg's female employees. The lower-

LOCAL BREVITIES

Yesterday, a young man, who, by the way has a perfect feminine face, called to his assistance some of Worth's imitators, togged himself in genuine lady's gear and proceeded to have some sport with the young men on the avenue. With flaxen bangs, a dainty cap, and swinging a parasol in one hand and a portmonnie [sic] in the other he sallied forth to the conquest, smiling lavishly upon the susceptible swains. From store to store she–that is, he–glided, receiving most polite attention from the single clerks–and some of the married ones, too. His triumphal march was cut short by one of the genuine fairer sex, who discovered his Adam's apple and gave him away, when he made swift steps for his home.

–Daily Ledger, May 17, 1885

class girls, known as crib girls, worked the lower floors, and the more expensive girls worked the upper floors. The city fined each woman $10 a month, and West Coast Wagon protested, saying, "Vile and lewd women are employed to draw custom[ers] for the bars; also…these women and vile and vicious men consort here. The women exhibit themselves at the windows dressed in an indecent and immodest manner…and the drunken orgies that occur there are frightful. There are employed a number of American, Japanese, French, Scandinavian and Negro prostitutes that stand at the doors and windows in a half nude condition."

Both the mayor and the city were saved from having to take action against Sandberg when, two months later, he bought the West Coast Wagon factory.

Peter Sandberg was becoming a very wealthy man He became influential in local politics and ran his nefarious businesses pretty much as he pleased. He married, had a daughter and lived in a nicely appointed home in Tacoma. He also owned property on Anderson Island and hired men who'd gambled away all their wages to clear the land there, build a house and plant an orchard. After acquiring the West Coast Wagon property, he was granted permission to excavate a cellar one hundred feet long and wide and ten feet deep under the factory. Well-known "gravel pirate C.D. Elmore did the work." Speculations as to its eventual use were rampant. Sandberg also added three floors and reopened the premises in 1902, amid much civic fanfare, as the Kentucky Liquor Company.

In 1901, he bought Tacoma Baths. His full-page newspaper advertisements claimed "the largest, finest and most complete assortment of the best known brands of Wines, Liquors and Cigars ever offered on Puget Sound." Members of the "Green Industry," i.e. loggers, were frequent guests. Underneath it on the Pacific Avenue side was said to be a barbershop operated by Gottlieb Jaeger.

However, Sandberg's days as the king of Fourteenth Street were numbered. At the instigation of the mayor, the city council passed an ordinance prohibiting treating in saloons "and gave financial support to do-gooders to clean up the city." Raiding and closing dives and state prohibition laws severely hindered Sandberg's ability to continue operating as he had. And trying his hand at other businesses, with which he had little or no experience, failed, costing Sandberg some of his properties.

When Peter Sandberg died on April 20, 1931, his estate was valued at $50,000.

With both Harry Morgan and Peter Sandberg dead, it might seem as if the city would clean up its act, but that wasn't going to happen anytime soon.

Chapter 10

WHAT'S A PORT WITHOUT SMUGGLING? AND WHAT'S SMUGGLING WITHOUT INCLUDING OPIUM?

*P*uget Sound is the third-largest estuary in the United States and has 170 islands in what is called the San Juan Group. Is it any wonder that smuggling was a lucrative business for many, especially after the 1882 Exclusion Act that blocked Chinese immigrants?

In 1880, 3,186 Chinese people lived legally in the state, and their communities often served as drop-off sites—places where the newly smuggled could blend in. And once they were "in," opium smuggling followed—not just for personal use but also to sell. As Seattle is north of Tacoma and closer to the San Juan Islands, it had more issues with smuggling and addiction than did Tacoma. But residents here were by no means immune to the problem. At the end of the nineteenth and turn of the twentieth century, problems regarding both smuggling and illegal use came fast and furious. One of the more unusual was reported by the *Tacoma Commerce* when, on December 19, 1886, Judge Greene (possibly Washington Territory chief justice of the Supreme Court) condemned the Oregon Railway and Navigation Company's steam vessel *Idaho* for engaging in opium smuggling.

Many of Tacoma's arrests were small potatoes: in September 1904, James Thomas, a local "dope fiend," stole a wheel (a bicycle) from a newspaper boy on Ninth and C Streets and rode away on it. He was sentenced to thirty days on the chain gang. In February 1910, customs officials confiscated twelve pounds of opium, tea sets, porcelain and three hundred pieces of silk from the *Surveric*, a British steamer. The silk was hidden in bags of rice, and the other items were scattered around the ship. According to Inspector Roy Ballinger, it was the crew's actions that led to the search.

In early October 1911, Sheriff Robert Longmire knew something was up when he found a broken window in the jail. The following night, he and a jailer hid outside and caught Robert L. Cooper in the act of climbing in and calling the prisoners, to whom he was selling opium and morphine tablets. Cooper was sentenced to thirty days.

User Frank Wilson was arrested in February 1912 when he bought, in order to resell, a large amount of cocaine from H.R. Coles, a Ruston drugstore owner. Wilson was fined $100, and Coles pleaded no contest. However, ship captain N. Kobayashi of the *Japanese Mexico Maru* protested his own innocence when his steward smuggled in 240 tins of opium. Then, a year later, Tacoma was shaken to its core when the *Times* reported that four hundred members of Tacoma's "smart set" (who knew Tacoma had a smart set?) were addicts.

On July 18, 1914, William Givens, a Black man, the former chef at the Tacoma Country and Gulf Club and proprietor of a notorious roadhouse, was given a preliminary hearing in federal court before U.S. commissioner McMillan and held over on a charge of having and transporting opium. According to authorities, "More opium is being brought into Tacoma than enters through all the California ports, Portland, Astoria and Seattle put together. It seems fully established that the route was from ocean liners, the drug being dropped overboard when they reach Tacoma, into launches, then to Chambers Creek by launch, then to Tacoma street cars, and then back into the city."

Givens had been a Tacoma resident for ten years and was considered by some to be the best chef in the city. After he left the country club, Givens became a private caterer, purchased a large touring car and was often seen driving members of the town's "Fashionable 400" (again, who knew there was a Fashionable 400?) out to the country, where he owned a house four miles from Sumner on the Stuck River. According to authorities, he'd opened a private opium den. When four deputy sheriffs raided his roadhouse, they found an iron spoon and half a pound of "smoking opium," several jars of the drug and a Chinese opium pipe. "I don't think there's any doubt that society girls were going out to the den," said a city detective. "It would not surprise me to hear that several prominent women and men, too, had been regular patrons of the opium joint. Givens is a notorious opium smoker and so is the white woman that he has been living with, Katherine Miller [or McCullouch]."

How drug fiends are getting forbidden drugs from crafty dealers. *Author's collection.*

Givens was reported to have been worth several thousand dollars and was expected to post the $1,700 bail. The *Seattle Daily Times* was particularly interested in the fact that the man owned seventeen "spick-and-span" suits, more than fifty silk shirts and "upwards of 100 ties." Unfortunately, as authorities raided roadhouses in Spanaway, Wilkeson, on American Lake and other places, the *Times* dropped the story. Not to worry, though, there were other stories to titillate the reader. White slavery was one, and one of the most notorious enslavers in Tacoma was a woman named Addie Swain.

Chapter 11

WHITE SLAVERY

The Addie Swain and Frederick LePlante Story

As if shanghaiing men off Tacoma's streets wasn't bad enough, nine months after the White-Slave Traffic Act was passed on June 25, 1910, an offshoot known as the National Purity League began, and within nine months, Tacoma women had started a branch. By that time, local papers had covered no fewer than six articles regarding the problem, the biggest being that of Frederick LePlante and Addie Swain.

Prior to her arrest in Tacoma on August 13, 1909, Addie Swain had been working in Seattle as a spirit medium and healer, trance seer, metaphysician who diagnosed diseases free of charge, astral seer medium and expert in Japanese hair removal. Seeking more lucrative grounds, she relocated to Tacoma and set up business as a palm reader in a small house on Seventeenth Street. Swain wasn't well known here, but she acquired a partner, Frederick LePlante, who had an ice cream parlor at 1718 Court C. The two were arrested on charges of "engaging in white slave traffic" and taken to jail on warrants issued by Deputy Prosecuting Attorney A.O. Burmeister based on evidence gathered by Detective C.P. Brady. The following day, they were arraigned and bound over for four days.

According to authorities, after a "reading," Swain would send young women looking for work to LePlante, who hired them, paying well, until "he succeeded in accomplishing their ruin." Swain may have been in jail, but she seemed to think her only charge would be vagrancy, and she talked willingly to reporters. She said she was fifty-three and was well known to police officers all along the coast. She told them that in 1897, when the

The white slave. *Puck* magazine cover. *Courtesy of the Library of Congress.*

Klondike gold rush was at its height, she left California and headed to Seattle and that, for a time, she made money posing as a trance medium and fortuneteller. She was nothing if not versatile. While in Seattle, she also called herself the proprietress of the Occult Hotel for workingmen, a pastor and offered (for a price) advice to those in need. At one time, she had been arrested for fraudulent use of the United States mail, and she once said her name was Swain-Seel. In December of the same year, she was kicked out of town and went to Vancouver, British Columbia, where, she said, she lived in a house on Seymour Street and was "in the clover for several months." Then, complaints about her reached the police, and "she skipped town so fast, she left nearly all her belongings behind." When authorities searched her house, the items included "apparatus used by fakers."

From Canada, Swain headed for Portland, where the chief of police told her "her absence would not lessen the attractions of the Oregon metropolis." That took her to Tacoma, then Spokane and then back to Tacoma.

"I've been in jail in nearly every city on the Pacific coast," she said, adding, "but they didn't get me in Vancouver, did they?"

Swain expected to be fined ten dollars, saying a week in jail would do her good because her stomach was out of order. She rattled on in this vein, and the paper promised court spectators a "whirlwind."

Both Swain and LePlante were in court on August 17, LePlante charged with engaging in white slave traffic. He asked for a change of venue, disappointing the throng of onlookers. Swain said she was not a fortuneteller; she was a psychologist and trance medium. The court postponed her trial until after LePlante's case had been resolved. Twelve years earlier, he had been convicted of incest in Jefferson County, Montana, and was sentenced to twenty years but paroled after ten. Now, the new charge meant he was considered to be a habitual criminal, and with a number of girls testifying against him, Frederick LePlante was convicted. In December, his attorney asked for a competency hearing, and his case was referred to the "lunacy commission." However, on Christmas Day, the judge sentenced him to not less than ten years nor more than fifteen at the Walla Walla State Penitentiary.

Deciding she liked the looks of jail food, Swain decided to plead guilty to fortunetelling, and that was all she was charged with. She served thirty days, returned to Seattle and resumed advertising her talents in the *Seattle Daily Times*. Her last ad in Seattle papers was in 1916.

Swain and LePlante may have disappeared from the streets of Tacoma, but white slavery hadn't.

April 1910 saw the arrest of A.O. (or O.N. or O.S.; the *Tacoma Times* reporter wasn't consistent) Sether, also known as "Pauley (or Polly) the hack driver." He was in jail on a white slavery charge along with Tracy (or Teresa) Hanson, age seventeen, and Maud Harrington, age nineteen, arrested for robbery and for being members of a disorderly house at 704 South E Street (or D Street) owned by Sether. The two women agreed to testify against Sether and to await grand larceny charges later. At Sether's June trial, three women testified, but the charges were dismissed. Sether stayed out of trouble until 1914, when he tried to buy a set of tools using a bogus check.

In early June 1910, Lily Morrill was in court facing charges of "aiding the white slavery traffic." According to a *Times* reporter, she looked much older than her thirty-five years. "Disease, fast living, late hours, stimulants and drugs" had each done a "part in making a wreck of the woman," he wrote. She sat in the courtroom, staring out the window until her name was called. In a monotonous voice, she pleaded guilty; with an expressionless face, she listened to her sentence. When Colonel J.J. Anderson ran in Tacoma for prosecuting attorney a few months after Morrill disappeared from history, he said, "Blind pigs [low-class drinking establishments] abound not only in this city, but in numerous places throughout the county; more than a score of regular games are running on Pacific avenue [*sic*], and the system of 'white slavery' that exists at Fourteenth and A streets is a disgrace to the community." Anderson lost, but he was right, as proven when, two months later, brothers Frank and Bob Snyder were arrested for bringing Nellie Anderson and Clara Morton down from British Columbia and holding them for white slavery.

However, let it not be said that all the women were victims. When an eighteen-year-old Tacoma girl named Emma Tamley (or Pearl Turner, according to the *Capital Journal*, an Oregon paper) brought charges against Peter Barbaraz, accusing him of hypnotizing her into a life of crime, the *Times* called her "pretty." By 1914, when she had broken her parole six times, she was merely "average." Barbaraz went to prison, but the Salvation Army stepped in to help Tamley, and the judge gave her a seventh chance.

Chapter 12

EVERY MILITARY BASE NEEDS A LITTLE "JOY"

t an election held on Saturday, January 6, 1917, Pierce County residents voted in favor of donating land south of Tacoma to the United States government to be used as an army post. On May 26, 1917, Captain David L. Stone and his staff arrived. The War Department named it Camp Lewis after the Lewis and Clark Expedition. Almost immediately, initial construction began; the work was being pushed forward because of World War I. A mere ninety days later, Camp Lewis was ready for occupancy. The first recruits started arriving in early September. Soon after, a "humdrum colony" of shacks began going up near the camp's entrance.

Three men—W.L. Blackburn, J.C. Bryn and a silent partner—rented approximately four acres adjacent to the camp from eight individual property owners and subleased lots to various proprietors who developed what became known as the Joy Zone.

According to the *Seattle Star*, "The street from Pacific Highway to Camp Lewis looked cheap and tawdry." The zone was said to resemble "a gold-rush mining town." At night and especially on weekends, it teemed with men who crowded the dusty, noisy street. Under glaring lights, they patronized hot dog stands, fruit vendors, an apple stand, a candy stand, a pool hall, restaurants and souvenir stands. Most of the businesses were legitimate, but several vice merchants used back rooms for illegal activities. A thriving bootlegging business operated from the beginning. On October 11, military police arrested alleged bootleggers B. Cecil Jackson of Everett, Jack Thompson

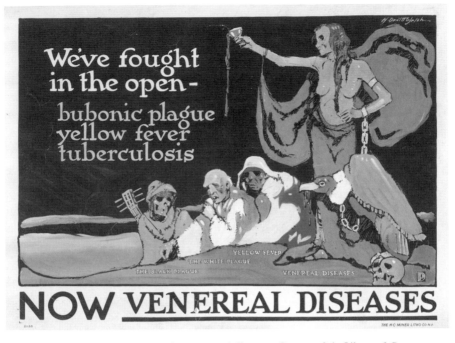

A government poster warning against venereal diseases. *Courtesy of the Library of Congress.*

and C. Thornton. Under a loose floorboard in the rear of Jackson's small stand, MPs found a stash of liquor. His account books indicated business had been good and that many of the recruits owed him money.

The services of a prostitute were also available. One night, while members of the secret service and military police watched, two cars driven by women picked up men from the Zone and took them to an undisclosed place farther down the road.

Since the Zone was on private property, Camp Commander Major General Henry A. Greene was initially unable to close it down, so he had it cordoned off instead. One by one, the concessionaires contacted Greene's aide, Captain Welty. "You knew that you would have to move in a short time anyway," Welty said. "The government will have control of the land from the county before the end of the week. Then you will have to move. In the meantime we can't close you up, but we can keep the soldiers out."

"We have been here twenty-four hours," a pretty girl in one stand said to her neighbor, "and now the boys dassant even smile at us—tough luck."

"Selling out at half-price," the pennant man shouted, but there were no takers.

On October 17, 1917, the military ordered the Joy Zone cordoned off. The blockade remained in place until late October, when the area was condemned, the shacks removed and the property incorporated into the camp. No one made the money they thought they would, and lawsuits immediately began. Attorney Govnor Teats, representing some of the defendants, asked if the shacks had increased or decreased the property's value. A representative for Pierce County said they had decreased values. Then lawyers on the same side began fighting among themselves. The trouble was that part of the team represented property owners, while others represented those who had leased the land and built the shacks. Part of the team wanted separate verdicts, and others didn't. Attorney P.C. Sullivan said separate verdicts would bring up unending side issues. He wanted one general award for each tract that would include the value of the land with any improvements. "The lease-holders," he said, "could fight anything else out with the property owners later." Representing both parties, Teats and his partner "Titlow" (probably Aaron Titlow) didn't know how to respond. At trial, the raised voices of everyone talking at once filled the courtroom. Finally, the judge stepped in and said the jury should bring in one verdict covering the total value of the property with improvements, if applicable. The leaseholders could then introduce evidence to show what they thought the value of their buildings might have been. Field marshal Scott Henderson, an enemy to both sides, "promised to introduce stipulations already entered into between the County and the property owners in which the County's figures were agreed to and no additional value was given for the temporary shacks." Peter Brohl, who owned land adjacent to Camp Lewis, said he had paid fifty-five dollars an acre for one piece of land and sixty dollars for another.

The jury, which had gone out to see the tract, rendered its verdict on October 29. The land was worth what the county said and in some cases slightly more.

While all this was going on, General Greene decided that Camp

VENEREAL DISEASE AT CAMP LEWIS, SEPTEMBER 21, 1917, TO MAY 31, 1918

Total number of cases: 3,697

Number of men already infected when received at camp: 3,505

Total number of cases developing after mustering in: 192

Number of men mustered in at Camp Lewis: 88,000

Percentage of infection among men arriving at camp: 4.2 per 1,000

After entering camp: 0.22 per 1,000

—Americanhistory.si.edu

Lewis needed a recreation park. The amusement grounds, named Camp Greene in his honor, had stores, bakeries, laundries, telephone exchanges, tailors, cobblers—everything needed for a soldier's health and comfort. The claim was that a soldier should have to look no farther than the camp for amusement.

But things were not yet over. Greene was accused of spending too much time and energy on the men's recreation and morals and not enough on their training. When the Ninety-First (the division from Camp Lewis) reached France, the men needed additional training. The major general was demoted to brigadier general, retired and died of a heart attack on August 19, 1921.

Of the Joy Zone's three promoters, the silent partner was considered a good, law-abiding Tacoma citizen who just "fell in with the other two." J.C. Bryan, who was wanted in connection with a white slave charge, disappeared. And W.L. Blackburn was taken to Seattle to answer a charge of forging and cashing checks and of skipping town with $500 from a trust fund.

A writ of garnishment was served on Sheriff Longmire in an attempt to force him to return $100 he found on Blackburn at the time of his arrest.

Two men who worked at the Joy Zone filed a suit against the partnership for $180 in back wages.

The one surviving building, which had become the Red Shield Inn, now serves as the Lewis Army Museum.

Chapter 13

JAIL BREAKS AND CHAIN GANGS

Mounted bandits made a futile attempt to hold up the Northern Pacific passenger train No. 4 from Portland, at Roy this morning. The station is 24 miles south of Tacoma, at the edge of the prairie....Seeing that their attempt was foiled the bandits quickly mounted their horses and rode away.
—Tacoma Times, January 2, 1904

As the 1880s and '90s advanced, good things were happening in Tacoma: the various outlying communities were being annexed; construction began on Annie Wright Seminary, Fannie Paddock Hospital and the Tacoma Hotel; telephones and gas lighting were introduced; Pacific Avenue was paved; and the first steamer from Asia arrived, bringing with it a future of international trade. But then, as now, newspapers loved to dwell on bad news. If you believed all you read, it seemed as if Tacoma couldn't catch a break. An epidemic of smallpox ran rampant through the town. There were so many fires, two of which were major, that construction of a better water system had to be rushed through to completion. Six men organized a syndicate and attempted to seize the tidelands. And in 1888, William Martin broke out of jail.

When Tacoma residents awoke on the morning of April 23, 1888, it was to the news that a murderer was on the loose. William Martin, on death watch for robbing and killing Old Town saloonkeeper Fred Neitzel, had broken out of the jail and was on the lam. People were warned to be on the lookout for a thirty-year-old man, five feet, seven and a half inches tall, with

Pacific Avenue, looking north from Thirteenth Street, circa 1907. *Courtesy of the Library of Congress.*

hazel eyes, auburn hair and almost completely white eyelashes, wearing a dirty gray shirt, dark coat and pants but no vest, hat or shoes. He had been in jail for four months to the day.

Tacoma had had a number of jails. The first, in 1874, was made of two-by-four planks "spiked together" and "located in the alley between the 2900 block of McCarver and Starr Streets in Old Tacoma; then at North 12th and G Streets, and then on a dock at the foot of Carr Street." The last police station in Old Town was on "the bay side of North 30th and Starr Streets." New Tacoma had a two-story wooden police station, which included a dog pound and police court, just east of A Street on South Twelfth. However, the one Martin broke out of was at South Eleventh and D (Market) Streets.

Around midnight on December 23, 1887, Martin had entered a tavern belonging to Fred Neitzel. So as not to alert Neitzel, Martin removed his shoes outside. But when the door closed behind him, Neitzel swung around with a lantern in his hand and went after the would-be robber. "I intended to tell him to throw up his hands," Martin later said, "but he was too quick for me and I had to shoot. I fired first over his head, thinking to scare him, but he grabbed for me and though I told him to keep back he wouldn't and I emptied my revolver, five shots. It was a Smith and Wesson, 45 caliber."

A police officer in the area who had heard the shots saw Martin running and fired several shots of his own, one of which hit the murderer in the shoulder. He kept running, though, and escaped into the woods. The next day, Martin was suffering so badly from the wound that he found "a shanty in the suburbs" and sent word to the police that he was ready to surrender. Once in jail, doctors gave him a fifty-fifty chance of surviving.

After his capture, Martin went on to say, "When he [Neitzel] fell, I turned down the lights and then went through his pockets for the safe keys. As I took them two or three dollars rolled on the floor but I paid no attention to them. The safe was open but the little drawers were locked and I was just getting at them when the bartender came in and I jumped through the window."

Neitzel had been well liked, and prior to his trial, Martin was taken to McNeil Island for his own protection. After his trial, he was transferred back to the South Eleventh and D Street jail to await hanging. In his cell, Martin was shackled around the ankles, with the shackles attached to a lightweight chain that was attached to a heavy-weight chain by a swivel, and that chain was stapled to the floor. Though Martin neither smoked nor chewed, the day guard gave him a cigar box of sand to use as a spittoon. When visitors arrived—a minister, a *Tacoma Daily Ledger* reporter to whom he'd promised a story and various ladies of the community to help him pray—Martin kept the box of sand under his blanket so no one would see that he had been using the sand to wear away the swivel.

On the night of the escape, guard H.L. Farley entered the twelve-by-fifteen-foot cell, gave the prisoner a nightlight and hunkered down in a corner for a smoke. Farley, who generally spent his days doing anything but sleeping, had that day been both target shooting and doing odd carpentry jobs. The activities took their toll; he fell asleep. That gave Martin the opportunity he needed to complete the swivel job uninterrupted. Once done, he walked out of the cell, locking the door behind him.

Farley later said that the sound of the cell door closing was what woke him and that he grabbed a broom, also in the cell, and began pounding on the ceiling to wake the deputies sleeping on the floor above. It took, he said, an hour to get their attention. Deputy Sheriff Calvin Wilt speculated that Farley actually just kept on sleeping after the jailbreak.

During what was left of that night, three things happened: Martin broke into a woodshed a block up the hill from the jail and used an axe to break the chain off the shackles. He kept the tool, found two left foot shoes of different sizes and was seen jumping various fences, hightailing it over the wharf to the water, eventually disappearing by boat. Sheriff Wilt, in the meantime, sent out telegrams trying to locate some tracker dogs, canvassed the business district for money to offer a reward and organized an official posse. And local men organized their own posse. Carrying knives, Winchester rifles and six-shooters, and wearing either Mexican cowboy attire or buckskins, they split up, staking out Steilacoom, where an old friend of Martin's lived and where they found but then lost the murderer's trail.

Eventually, Farley took to his bed, full of narcotics and under a doctor's care, and after the deputy sheriff and his men accused each other, blame fell on Wilt because there had been seven previous jail escapes and two suicides on his watch. The general public didn't care one way or another. Most people were just irked about the length of time it took for word of the escape to be made public.

Neither posse ever found Martin, though they did find his well-provisioned shack down near the smelter. As for Martin himself, ten days after the escape, reports came back that he'd been spotted in North Yakima, where he'd bought a horse off an Indian before heading north into the Okanagan country. Four years after his escape, Martin was spotted in New Westminster, British Columbia, but from there he disappeared.

His was not the first jailbreak, and they continued to be a problem.

Two months before Martin's escape, an ex–grocery man named Frank Granville made a less successful break for freedom. He hightailed it for Victoria but was captured two days later at Port Townsend carrying cash and checks totaling $5,000.

As well as men, teenage boys were often a problem. In fact, in 1915 the *Tacoma Times* said child-perpetrated crimes were raging in the city.

When Martin J.B. Johnson's store was robbed in February 1912, three of the "youthful" burglars—Fred Folson, Sylvester Cooper and Paul Maleski— along with Earl Myers, who was being charged with stealing a motorcycle in Seattle, all broke out of jail. They were "confined in an ordinary room" on the second floor that had barred windows and a door with bars over a fourteen-inch hole. While the jailer was out with the patrol wagon, the

Tacoma's finest at the turn of the century.

Tacoma's finest at the turn of the century. *Author's collection.*

boys ripped the bars off the door and escaped through the jailer's office. According to the *Tacoma Journal*, "The six-celled city jail was in deplorable condition. It was old and dilapidated and not strong enough to hold ordinary vagrants and petty thieves. At the time of construction, the building material used was simply a double thickness of thin boarding…that could be cut through without much difficulty." Also, "during the daylight hours, up to eight o'clock at night, the prisoners were allowed access to the main lobby." As if to prove the *Journal*'s observation, another break was attempted in June.

In 1892, prisoner Arthur Kuhl, Peter Sandberg's accountant and a convicted white slaver, was a trusted prisoner. At the time of his arrest, Kuhl's aging fox terrier, Beauty, wanted to stay with her master. When a jailer tried to force her out, "he nearly lost the seat of his pants." One day, Kuhl was sent to open a window and Beauty accompanied him. While poking around in a padded cell, she climbed onto a window ledge. Kuhl went to see what she was up to and, while climbing out onto the ledge, found three small steel saws, a set of wire cutters and a set of plyers wrapped in paper from Washington Hardware, all stashed under a pile of leaves. Kuhl took the tools to the head jailer. The assumption was they were placed on the wrong windowsill.

Pierce County jailer James Longmire foiled the next escape attempt. On November 30, 1912, he overheard a conversation between prisoner E.

Salyards and another inmate that made him suspicious. Later that night, Longmire hid in a wood pile behind the jail and saw Salyards cut an eighteen-inch hole in a window screen. Then, using a knife made into a saw, he spent an hour cutting on the bars while two other prisoners stood guard. After Longmire stopped the attempted escape and put Salyards in solitary, Prosecuting Attorney Lorenzo Dow recommended a ten-year sentence for the criminal, who had been convicted of forging a $5,000 bank draft from a Tacoma bank.

In those days, the Pacific Northwest was not without the occasional gun battle. One involved ringleader Tom French, aka Jack Lawn, aka George Miller; his partner George Hubbard; and three other convicts, all of whom escaped from the Pierce County jail at midnight on January 4, 1918. The jailbreak caused the same kind of excitement in Tacoma as when Ted Bundy escaped from the Pitkin County courthouse in Aspen, Colorado.

In December, a jury had found French guilty of robbing the Buckley Hardware Store in Buckley, Washington. He had already served two terms in the Walla Walla Penitentiary and was wanted for burglary in Wenatchee. He was out on patrol when he robbed the hardware store. Between his trial and actual incarceration, French approached a man named George Pidd and told him he planned to escape. French had sworn never to return to Walla Walla. Pidd—a private in the Forty-Fourth Infantry at Camp Lewis who had been sentenced by court-martial to life in prison for using a lead pipe on a Camp Lewis jitney driver named Lawrence Berquist—felt the same way. While in jail, French got hold of an old syrup pitcher and wrapped it in a sock. At 6:00 p.m. on the night of the escape, when jailer E.D. Christy let some of the prisoners out of their cells, French slipped out of his unnoticed and hid on top of Pidd's cell at the far corner of what was called the state tank, defined as "a holding area where arrestees were held while waiting to be processed." He stayed there until midnight, when Jailer Peter McCabe relieved Christy. Some of the men, who were by then back in confinement, said they wanted to go to the toilet, and Pidd said he had a letter he wanted sent to his wife. McCabe approached Pidd's cell, and French jumped him, knocking him unconscious with the syrup pitcher. The two tied the jailer's hands to the cell bars, and French took the jailer's revolver, leather strap for "handling insane prisoners" and keys and went down the line unlocking cell doors. "You can get out but don't try to follow me," he said. "I'll kill the first one of you who makes a disturbance." He then worked for half an hour but was unable to open Pidd's cell door.

Back on the evening of December 27, outside accomplices William Allen and George Spencer had stolen a car parked at 5027 South M Street that belonged to C.F. Gillett and stashed it "at a hidden location convenient for the jail break but somewhere out of sight." Now on the lam, French hopped in the car accompanied by John Johnson, accused of robbing a post office in North Yakima; nineteen-year-old Arthur Grier; and Sam Suddoch and headed south.

If Judge D.B.D. Smeltzer can find no prohibiting statute, all women hereafter convicted in his court of aggravated offenses, will, in default of payment of the fine, be required to don bloomers and take their places in the chain gang with the male prisoners.

—Topeka State Journal, August 8, 1911

The prostrate McCabe was found about 1:30 a.m. and taken to Tacoma General. French's blows had been so violent that McCabe needed twenty-four stitches. Pidd was put "in the black hole," and while a posse of heavily armed deputy sheriffs scoured both Tacoma and outlying areas, word of the escape went out to various law enforcement offices around the state.

At 11:00 a.m., the men were spotted near a Kelso garage where they had stopped for repairs. Having been advised to be on the lookout, local marshal Ed Hull and "a volunteer helper," a logger named Carl Hays, captured Johnson. When Hull ordered the others to stop where they were, French pulled out his gun and opened fire. Hull shot it out of his hand, and when French bent to pick it up, the marshal fired again, shooting French through the neck. French went down, and the other two men took off. Kalama sheriff Clark Studebaker picked up Arthur Grier.

Arthur Grier was charged with burglary and perjury.
George Spencer, the car thief, was found guilty of aiding and harboring an escapee and heavily fined.
William Allen, Spencer's partner, was given a suspended sentence.
Tom French was given two months to live; his date of death is unknown.
Sam Suddoch disappeared.

During those early years in Tacoma's history when jailbreaks were common, some of the city fathers tried to keep the prisoners busy working on chain gangs. When, in May 1886, Mayor Jacob Mann decided Pacific Avenue needed a little TLC, he sent a chain gang to clean out the stagnant gutters and pools of standing water and remove loose stones and general debris. However, the idea of using men joined together by balls and chains

No way to escape. *Courtesy of the Library of Congress.*

to help with city projects found disfavor with some people. "The men are being subjected to ridicule," they said, "by being forced to exhibit themselves publically." As a result, chain gangs came and went.

Vagrants Harvey Garrison and Paul McLaughlin worked five days on a chain gang in late March and early April 1904. But four months later, when a Norwegian man named Andrew Hanson Frederick Ole Hole was also charged with vagrancy, he was sentenced to work on what was called a "street squad." That euphemism didn't last; the following month, when the previously mentioned James Thomas, "dope fiend" and thief, was sentenced to thirty days, the words "chain gang" were back.

In trying to prune the city's budget, Mayor Angelo Fawcett said, "If the city is going to be hard up next year [1916] we can easily make the chain gang do street cleaning work. After a man gets out of jail nowadays, he's soft and fat from just resting so comfortably, and he is in no fit condition to go back to work."

City prisoners were put to work, but instead of being chained, a man was assigned to keep an eye on them.

Part III

THE COCKSURE ERA

Chapter 14

A NEW CENTURY

The year 1910 was a census year; on April 15 and for the next twenty-five days, enumerators (census takers) counted Tacoma's population. Their tally came to between 109,000 and 110,000. In August, an agent came to town, rechecked the figures and reduced the number to 106,400. Residents protested and demanded another recount. In December, a second agent arrived, checked the figures turned in and reduced the number to 83,743. Up and down the Pacific coast, cities were under investigation, charged with padding their numbers. Fifteen Tacoma men pleaded guilty to padding and were fined fifty dollars each plus costs. Nevertheless, that was good growth for a city only thirty-five years old.

The turn of the century ushered in a period of time called the Cocksure Era. Thanks to the Klondike Gold Rush, Tacoma was smaller than Seattle, but it was no longer a frontier town. Downtown had three department stores: Rhodes Brothers and Stone Fisher on Broadway and the People's Store on Pacific Avenue. Puget Sound National Bank, built in 1910, was the tallest building west of the Missouri River.

The Domestic Bakery Company was on South Tenth Street, Sunrise Bakery was on K Street and Dickson Bros. Bakery/Matthaei Bread Company was on Eleventh Street and Tacoma Avenue, at the same address where Mars Bars were developed circa 1914.

The National Guard Armory opened its doors on New Year's Eve 1908 with a military ball. While some men were laying pipes in South Tacoma, others were sluicing out Old Woman's Gulch prior to building Stadium

It was counting day for the birds

Census day. *Author's collection.*

Bowl. A massive "Watch Tacoma Grow" banner could be seen from Commencement Bay's Commercial Dock. Actor Bing Crosby was born, and bicycling was all the rage. In fact, the Tacoma Wheelmen's Bicycle Club connected Delin Street with a path leading to the Hood Street reservoir near Holy Rosary Church.

This was a particularly exciting time for women, who were beginning to gain freedoms. Out with the corset, in with the brassiere; forget churning butter, women preferred to golf, hike and ride bikes. Instead of marrying young, they were working in offices, shops and factories and welcomed an American invention, the blouse, which was worn with a skirt. These freedoms were not without their dangers, though. Many young women were

The new woman and her bicycle. There will be several varieties of her. *Courtesy of the Library of Congress.*

unaware of the menaces around them—and not without cause. There was a prevailing fear that women who appeared in public without men were in danger of being forced into prostitution by gangs who trafficked in young girls. Tacoma was accused of becoming a headquarters of vice in the Northwest. The *Tacoma Times* claimed that Seattle was sending its prostitutes here "in hordes. Crooks and white slavers are flocking to Tacoma where the police department has thrown down the bars and given free license to do business." The mayor made no attempt to deny the facts but said the situation was the police's responsibility. From Fourteenth Street to Fifteenth Street, from A Street to Court A, ladies of the night plied their trade with little interference. However, sometimes peril started out as something innocent.

Chapter 15

A CULT MOVES IN

The Washington Colony was "a group of utopian Kansans" who arrived in the state in 1881, took up residence in Whatcom County and reestablished the old mill on Whatcom Creek. It became known as the Colony Mill. What is now Burley, Washington, began in 1898 as a "cooperative socialist colony [started] by a group called the Co-operative Brotherhood." A year earlier, the Brotherhood had established the Equality Colony in Skagit County. Not to be left behind, Tacoma was going to get a colony, too, when a man named the Reverend Albert Dahlstrom arrived in town with plans to launch the Helga Colony, which was actually more of a cult than a colony. The difference is that a colony is "a group of people who moved to a new place but remain culturally attached to their original" home, and a cult is a diverse group of people with "a religious, philosophical or cultural identity." Cult members are usually fringe members of society, and Dahlstrom was certainly on the fringe.

Information about his background is scanty. Dahlstrom was born in Sweden and first appears in 1891 newspapers when he was preaching at the Swedish Baptist Church in Minnesota's Indian Lake Township. For the next few years, he "sermonized" in both Minnesota and Illinois—apparently without causing problems. However, all that changed when he confessed to "ruining" fifteen-year-old Annie Hagstrand, saying King David had done worse and been forgiven by God so he, Dahlstrom, also expected to be forgiven.

From then on, Dahlstrom fought the law until the law won. He was regularly referred to as an evangelist, a Mormon or a Lutheran minister and by himself as a Messenger of God. In 1906, he joined forces with Carl Mattson to create the Helga cult; its major tenet was polygamy. On March 1, 1907, Marie Pederson accused Dahlstrom of abducting her seventeen-year-old daughter, Martha, and taking her to a hotel "for the purpose of concubinage." Dahlstrom was arrested, but the charges had to be dropped because Martha disappeared. Eventually, she wrote a letter explaining her actions, and Dahlstrom immediately divorced his apparently unknown or at least unmentioned first wife and married Martha, incurring contempt of court charges. Soon after, while he was in the hospital recovering from varicole surgery (a varicole is "an enlargement of the veins within the loose bag of skin that holds the testicles/scrotum,") Chicago preachers learned about a young Denver girl who had fathered Dahlstrom's child. For whatever reason, the "Denver" story faded away, and Dahlstrom was soon acquitted of Martha's abduction. He continued preaching in Minnesota and Illinois and, at the same time, worked to establish his colony. However, in November 1913, he and Martha were in Snohomish, Washington, where Martha sued him for divorce, claiming abandonment and cruelty, and asked for possession of their two children. December 22 found Dahlstrom in a Tacoma court accused of white slavery by Tacoma girl Edna Englund. W.W. Wingard, manager of the Northwest Detective Agency, who had been trying to find Edna's sister, Clara, lured the reverend to Tacoma, and Dahlstrom was arrested at the corner of Eleventh and Pacific Avenue. Fred L. Boalt, a *Tacoma Times* reporter, had a field day covering the story.

Dahlstrom's crime was "using his cult," which had a branch at Everett, as a cloak for running away with nineteen-year-old Edna (sometimes called Elnona), who had lived with her parents at 4101 McKinley Avenue, and of hiding her older sister, Clara (sometimes called Hilda).

According to the *Times*, he "had 27 wives in different parts of Washington, in Fresno, California and in Minneapolis, had fathered children with seven of them, and often chose women from the most attractive members of his cult. 'I received a Heavenly message ordering me to select new wives,'" he would tell them. Brigham Young explained his having fifty-five wives by espousing a similar philosophy.

Dahlstrom relocated, more or less permanently, to Washington in 1912 and met Englund at a church meeting. He told her the lord had advised him to take her as a wife. Telling her parents they were legally married, the pair headed for Fresno and was joined by Clara, with whom Dahlstrom was maintaining a clandestine correspondence. From there, they went to Minneapolis, where Dahlstrom told Edna that the lord had told him to take another wife. When she protested, he told her she would be left out in the cold if she didn't keep quiet. Dahlstrom then took Edna to his Everett farm to meet Martha, who, needless to say, wasn't pleased. However, after working his powers of persuasion, Martha agreed to the unorthodox arrangement.

What's more exciting than a new spouse? While traveling to Minnesota, Dahlstrom began ignoring Edna. To stop her complaining about the situation, he bought her a ticket back to Tacoma. Once home, she told her parents she'd been a slave to Dahlstrom, and that's when they hired Detective Wingard to find Clara. Writing to her parents, Clara said, "There is no use to come home now; all is over." The papers don't say where Martha was during all this.

Edna was supposed to keep quiet about the situation, but that didn't happen. Dahlstrom was arrested in 1913 and in court on December 22. Boalt described him as "tall and slim and having a meek expression and irresolute and ill-regular features," adding that when he spoke, Dahlstrom's manner became "didactic and a bit pompous." He talked about how many books he'd written, how many converts he'd made and how successful he'd been. Regarding Martha, he said he'd been wed before and didn't wait for the divorce to become final before marrying Martha, so he didn't think the marriage was legal. He said he had, in fact, bought the tickets to Fresno but that he and Edna didn't share a berth, at which statement Edna called him a liar. Under threat of being removed from court, she, with obvious difficulty, was forced to remain quiet.

Dahlstrom's attorney said Martha and her mother had been seen at the Englund home and that the whole thing was a conspiracy. However, when asked if he preached polygamy, Dahlstrom said yes, but only for European women, and that it would cure prostitution.

After a hearing, Dahlstrom went before a United States commissioner and pleaded not guilty to having more wives than he was entitled to. "I'm not sure I have one wife," he said, "let alone twenty-seven." Nevertheless, he was held on $5,000 bail.

During the trial, Edna said she had first heard Dahlstrom preach at a place across the street from her home, that she didn't know what denomination he was and that he preached "Jesus was the foundation of all religion. The whole family became interested in him," she said, "and he was often at their home, also that Dahlstrom owned up to having a wife, Martha, on his farm near Everett but that they weren't really married. He wanted me for his wife," Edna said, "but there wasn't really a ceremony because it wasn't necessary."

As it turned out, Detective Wingard wasn't the only person looking into Dahlstrom's activities. E.O. Sawyer, a *Times* special correspondent, contacted Martha Dahlstrom, who told him, "When I heard he was arrested, I was so glad I didn't know whether to laugh or cry. When I think of all the grief and tears that man brought to girls and women through his preaching and practicing polygamy it makes me desperate." She also said that before her, a woman named Minnie Jensen had been his female companion and that she, Martha, had knowledge of sixteen plural wives but had heard of others.

Back in Tacoma, the commissioner said there was sufficient evidence to require the opinion of a grand jury. Dahlstrom couldn't make bail, as he was being harassed by creditors and was encumbered with mortgages. He spent Christmas in jail.

The trial ended in March, and Dahlstrom was found guilty of one count of violating the Mann White Slave Act. He was given a five-year sentence to be served on McNeil Island. He appealed and in July jumped bail and disappeared.

In February 1915, he was seen in Sweden.

In 1931, Swedish officials arrested him for giving anti-religion lectures.

Martha Dahlstrom was granted a divorce and awarded several thousand dollars' worth of community property.

Chapter 16

ELECTRICITY

It Transforms Lives

*B*y 1883, Tacoma's population of four thousand was six times what it had been in 1878. Though Thomas Edison's invention of the incandescent light was generating interest in easy access to electricity, Tacoma was dealing with a typhoid epidemic and had to clean up its water. Not until 1886 did a small powerhouse in Gallagher Gulch near Pacific Avenue and South Twenty-Sixth Street begin lighting the city. Initially, the lights weren't bright enough, there weren't enough of them around town and there was no lack of power shortages. According to the *Tacoma Commerce*, lamps for arc lighting of two thousand candlepower were in position on Pacific Avenue on April 23, 1887. All that was needed was a better engine to supply said power. When the lights were finally turned on ten months later, the candlepower was much less than originally stated.

Water and electricity fought for precedence until "American troops came marching home from World War I" and electricity had caught the public interest to such an extent that a commission was created by the New York legislature "to ascertain the most humane and practical method for criminal executions…sending out circulars requesting answers as to the modes of killing by electricity, poison, the guillotine, the garrote."

Electricity had arrived, but not without problems—just ask Joseph Adams, a lineman who fell from the top of a telegraph pole on January 16, 1904, after getting zapped with "a heavy shock of electricity." A *Tacoma Times* reporter said the fall and the shock might have "disabled" an ordinary man, but the only effect on Adams was to knock the breath out of him.

Snoqualmie Falls Power Company transfer house at Nineteenth and Jefferson Streets, 1902. *Courtesy of the Library of Congress.*

Manuel King, a miller for the Albers Brothers Milling Company, also received a shock. He was placing a new fuse in the safety apparatus connected with the motor used in the mill and accidentally touched the fuse and the ground wire simultaneously. The five hundred volts of electricity knocked him unconscious and made his body "so stiff and rigid his fellow employees thought he was dead." An ambulance was called, but by the time it arrived, he had recovered enough to go home. It was expected he would be back to work the following day. These two accidents were operator errors; not so the deaths on February 1, 1909, of Arthur W. Charlson and John R. Ohrstrom.

Twenty-four-year-old Charlson, a blacksmith working for West Coast Wagon Company, and forty-five-year-old Ohrstrom, head shipping clerk for the Younglove Grocery Company, were killed when eleven hundred volts of electricity passed through their bodies.

It was 7:00 a.m., and the two men had each turned on the lights at their respective places of employment when they were accidentally electrocuted. Both businesses were on Pacific Avenue; the wagon company's address was from no. 1948 to no. 1950 and the grocery company from no. 1932 to no.

The west side of Pacific Avenue. *Right to left*: 1920–22, Wiegal Candy Company Factory (1904); 1924–26, the Campbell Building (Davis Building) (1890); 1928–30, the Reese-Crandall and Redman Building (1890); 1932–36, the McDonald and Smith Building (1890); 1938–48, the F.S. Harmon Company Warehouse (1908). *Courtesy of the Library of Congress.*

1936. In between the two was the Harmon Building. A heavy power line with a city feed wire crossing in front of the Harmon Building, at the time under construction, caused the tragedy.

B. Hanson, a fellow employee, found Charlson underneath a light socket in the rear of the building. "The bulb had been wrenched from its fastenings as though the man had gripped it before becoming unconscious," papers said. For a brief time, Charlson hovered between life and death, and then death won.

Down the street, Ohrstrom was electrocuted when he turned the button of an electric globe in the shipping room. The doctors who had tried unsuccessfully to save Charlson were summoned and worked over Ohrstrom for more than an hour, but he died shortly after 10:00 a.m.

Meanwhile, the force of a shock from an incandescent socket knocked Charles Reid, another of the wagon company's blacksmiths, to the ground. At the same time, A.H. Frost, a clerk for the Armour Company at 1928–30

Pacific Avenue, walked into a smoky room. In trying to locate the source of the problem, he reached for the light socket, and the resulting shock sent him staggering to the floor.

The switches were turned off and the fire department notified. At 9:00 a.m., when the chemical fire extinguisher wagon arrived, hot wires at the Armour Building were still smoldering, and several pieces of lumber were knocked loose and later fell from the Harmon Building onto electrical wires. Also, the woodwork had become inflamed. A city electrician said the weight of the wood caused high-tension wires to swing clear of the cross-arm. It later sagged and came down, making contact with other wires. Constant rubbing of the two wires wore through their coatings, and the currents crossed. Except for the two casualties, the overall damage was considered to have been slight, though it was estimated that a great deal of wiring at the various buildings would have to be replaced.

The day before the accident, "a short current" had been discovered but not turned off. "It should have been as soon as the fact was known," various electricians said. According to the *Tacoma Times*, they felt the city should be held responsible.

City electrician Felix H. Lauson, when "told of the trouble on The Bismarck high tension wire, which was diverted into the 110 volt city feed wire," sent gangs of men out to investigate. Some called this a folly, claiming, "No efficient electrician would have dared to investigate a treacherous wire holding 2,200 volts. Instead, they would have used a magneto-bell. If it determines that a ground exists, the bell will ring. And if it did ring, the electrician would immediately cut the circuit."

Two days after the accident, attorneys were getting ready to take action against the city. G.D. Shaver, the coroner, however, took a peculiar position. "Since the circumstances surrounding the tragic deaths…would probably be recited in the superior court room," he said, he "saw no reason why the county should bear the expense of an official investigation.…No criminal carelessness could be shown in either of the cases, and they…are therefore matters to be settled by civil court instead of criminal actions."

Knowledge that the electricity was grounded at some unknown point was considered sufficient evidence of carelessness on behalf of the city, and because Tacoma citizens demanded it, Shaver empaneled a jury to hold an inquest. It began on February 4, the same day Ohrstrom's funeral was held at the Danish Lutheran Church on South Thirteenth and L Streets. At the proceedings, Lauson and six linemen and trouble-shooters were questioned. Lauson brought a mockup of the three buildings involved and said he had sent out a dozen linemen to locate the problem. The linemen "testified that they had searched the high tension wire from the 19th Street power station as far as Bismarck [Sixty-Fourth and McKinley] and had failed to find any crossed wires." C.J. Wilts, a bartender at the Rheim Hotel across the street from the three buildings, told of seeing "the crossed wires in front of the Harmon Building at 10:00 p.m. the night before the accident" and that they were emitting "large, hissing sparks." Other linemen said following the deaths they found "a primary wire rubbing against a secondary wire near the transformer at 12th and Pacific and the point of contact was clearly visible." Some linemen said they were not really sure whether these problems were strong enough to kill someone, and others refused to take the stand. The city's attorney claimed that "the inquest was a piece of folly, and that it would be used as a basis for [future] damage suits to be made against the city."

In all, after some twenty witnesses had been examined, the jury concluded that the deaths were accidental; criminal responsibilities against all parties involved were dismissed.

John Ohrstrom's wife, mother of their two children, filed a claim against the city, asking for $30,000 in damages. The claim was referred to the city's claims committee and was expected to be rejected because the accident was deemed not to be the city's fault. However, $27,000 in damages was eventually awarded. In August, a superior court jury reduced the amount to $18,000. Eleven months after the accident, the State Supreme Court further reduced the amount to $12,000 (approximately $349,288.35 in 2021 currency).

And that's where it remained.

Chapter 17

A LOVE TRIANGLE
ENDS IN MURDER

*S*hortly after midnight on the evening of May 14, 1909, five gunshots and a bang on the head killed Martin Kvalshaug. At South Puget Sound Avenue and Twelfth Street, a man named Charles Newcomb stepped out from his hiding place and fired three shots. Someone screamed, and then two more shots were discharged. The murder happened while Charles and his wife, Martina, were walking to their home at 1507 South Puget Sound (a short street off South Union) after a dance. Police officer J.E. Darnell and a man named J.S. Webb, who heard the shots, were the first on the scene and found the dead man. Leaving Kvalshaug where he fell, they went to the Kvalshaug home and found Mrs. Martina Kvalshaug and her sister-in-law, Mrs. George Dilley. Martina told them she knew what had happened to her husband but had no idea who could have shot him. She returned with them to where her husband's body lay and, according to Darnell, became "quite excited." From the murder site, she was arrested and taken to the jail to make a statement. Martina Kvalshaug would be held in jail for one year, eight months and fifteen days, and her trials became media sensations as far as local newspapers went.

Three months later, on October 27, a venire (panel) of 270 talesmen (prospective jurors) was called; the vetting process held the trial up for six days. Though no spectators were allowed during jury selection, people tried to crowd in anyway, and ropes were stretched diagonally across the corridor to keep them back. At the trial, Darnell said he was a few blocks away talking to Webb when they heard the rapid-fire shots, followed by a woman's scream and then the two additional shots. He thought two different people had fired the gun. Webb's testimony was identical to that of Darnell, but he did add that they had watched the streets for some time, eventually meeting Charles Newcomb, who, after identifying himself, was allowed to continue on to his home at 3716 South K Street (M.L. King Street).

As the trial entered its thirteenth day, an unruly mob, estimated to be 75 percent women, jammed the courthouse until it was necessary to call on the entire sheriff's department for crowd control; force became necessary. Once all who could found places in the courtroom, more than two hundred people were left standing in the corridors.

TWO STRINGS TO HER BOW

Two strings to her bow. *Courtesy of the Library of Congress.*

After Darnell and Webb testified, a Mrs. Thomas Battee took the stand. She said on the night of the shooting she sat next to Martina at the dance (held at the Pallies Hall, a substantial building extending from no. 762 to 774 South Thirty-Eighth Street). Newcomb and the defendant talked, and she said to him, "You had better go now."

Then Mamie Clark was sworn in. She said that at about ten o'clock one night while walking toward home with Martina, they cut down a dark trail and heard something moving in the brush. "Knowing about Martin's jealousy of Newcomb, I remarked that I thought it was Martin," and "Mrs. Kvalshaug agreed with me and said that he would get his head shot off prowling around in the brush spying on her."

The police captain testified that he had told Newcomb that Kvalshaug had "come through" (confessed) because he wanted Newcomb "to holler" (make a clean breast of things). The jury was instructed not to consider the confession as evidence against Mrs. Kvalshaug.

Initially, and over the objection of his court-appointed attorney, Charles Newcomb's admission of guilt was allowed and read to the jury. It said that he and Mrs. Kvalshaug had "a carefully pre-arranged plan," that he fired the first shots and dropped the gun and then she picked it up and fired the last ones. The court ruled that Newcomb had "to be found guilty before Mrs. Kvalshaug could be found guilty of being his accomplice."

On November 15 at 10:30 a.m., twenty-five-year-old Martina Kvalshaug took the stand. Papers said she wore a plain black dress and was quite attractive. She said she'd been born in South Dakota, had very little education and married at age seventeen. She and her husband moved to Tacoma in 1903, and she met Charles Newcomb at a dance in January. She admitted to having had a relationship with Newcomb but denied firing any shots. She said she'd eventually grown "tired of Newcomb and had decided to get rid of him because he had declared that he would knock her husband's block off." This statement was confirmed by Mrs. Clark. Mrs. Kvalshaug also said that in late March, she'd been in Fannie Paddock Hospital for two weeks and that Newcomb visited her, telling her he had received a letter that frightened him and asking for money "to buy a gun as he was afraid to go unarmed and had no money." He showed her the letter, and she didn't recognize the handwriting but did lend him ten dollars. After she was discharged from the hospital, Newcomb went in for an appendectomy and was there for two weeks. After his release, he wanted her to meet him at the Davenport Hotel on C Street (Broadway), and she declined. They did meet at Point Defiance, and she asked for her money back. Then, on May 14, they met at the Davenport after all. When asked why, she said she needed to tell him she wanted nothing more to do with him. She said she told him he'd been making a scene at the hall and her husband had refused to let the two dance. Newcomb, she said, asked her to leave Martin. She told him to quit such talk, that she would never leave her husband or children. She thought he was still at the dance when she and her husband left.

She also testified that while walking home on the night of the murder, she and her husband turned onto the trail at Twelfth and Puget Sound, and her husband stopped (no reason given) while she went on. When she heard the shots, she screamed, dashed back and saw a man running toward Twelfth Street. "I said, 'dear, can I do anything?' He shook his head very slightly, and then I put his hat on his chest and ran as fast as I could toward the home of the Dillies."

Throughout her incarceration, Mrs. Kvalshaug was said to have remained composed, reading and talking cheerfully to the jailers. "I know I am innocent and God will protect me," she said. However, she broke into tears twice: once when she received a scribbled note from her daughter, Evelyn, expressing her "great desire to see her soon," and again four weeks later when she was told that her children had been taken east to live with her mother-in-law.

The trial ended on November 20 and went to the jury at 3:10 p.m. While Kvalshaug spent a sleepless night in her cell, a few people remembered that there was a transom on the second floor and went up there to look down and spy on the jurors. They said that some of the men paced, some took their coats off, some made impassioned gestures and some shook their heads. At times, tempers flared to the point where the spies thought there would be fistfights. Nineteen hours and twenty-one votes later, the judge was told they were unable to reach a verdict. And so the accused was returned to her cell to await a second trial.

Jury selection for the next trial began on April 4, 1910. Ninety-nine men were called to create a panel of fourteen. Testimonies followed the same path as before, with one exception: H.C. Stevens, a professor of the University of Washington's psychology department, took the stand and said that because of Mrs. Kvalshaug's mental and physical condition directly following the murder, "it would have been possible for her to give an untrue confession. She would give answers suggested by her questioner without reasoning, in her mind, that such answers were not true."

When, on May 8, after eight hours of deliberations, the second jury was unable to reach a verdict, the judge sent them back to try again. The results were the same, and on December 27, the prosecuting attorney announced his decision to try the case a third time.

During the first two trials, defense attorneys protested the all-male juries. Women wanted to serve. But according to the *Seattle Daily News*, their letters to the Pierce County prosecutor said that they "want[ed] a chance to send the woman to the gallows or prison." So 180 tales*men* were called, with nary a woman in sight.

The third Kvalshaug trial began on January 13 and went to the jury at 9:15 p.m. on the twenty-second. This time, spectators were less interested in the verdict than they were in a charge made by her attorney "that a member of the prosecuting attorney's office had sequestered a witness material to the defense." If he was referring to Fred Geiger, who had told two different stories, the charge was true. Bearing this in mind, two days later jury spokesman C.E. Drowley said, "The mere fact that the prosecution was shown to have tampered with one of the witnesses was sufficient to supply the reasonable doubt."

Martina Kvalshaug was released.

On September 27, 1912, she was denied custody of her children by courts in South Dakota.

On December 21, 1912, she married a farmer named Just Peterson in Irene, Yankton County, South Dakota.

BUT WHAT OF HER ALLEGED ACCOMPLICE?

After he was found guilty in October 1909, Charles Newcomb was held in Pierce County jail for four years and six months. It was a record in both Pierce and King Counties. While there, he was a model prisoner. "He became jailer Thomas Desmond's right hand man, having full charge of everything inside the jail, including the maintenance of discipline among prisoners, the enforcement of the rules and the like," said the *Seattle Daily News*. The paper went on to say that Newcomb "carried all the keys except the one to the barred entrance gate" and that "no other prisoner has ever been so trusted in the Pierce County jail."

There was good news/bad news for Newcomb's future; when he filed for an appeal, his attorney failed to deposit the required court fees, and the appeal was thrown out. The attorney was later disbarred on other charges. But Washington's lieutenant governor, Louis F. Hart, commuted Newcomb's sentence to life in prison.

Before heading for Walla Walla, the prisoner bid his wife a final farewell. Mrs. Newcomb had stood fast in her loyalty, going so far as to sell their house to provide funds for her husband's defense. Newcomb, however, had come to the conclusion that her loyalty was blighting her life. "You are a young woman," he said, "and entitled to happiness for the rest of your life."

Before being taken to Walla Walla in autumn 1913, Newcomb made one last statement: "I shall go to Walla Walla unafraid. I shall obey the rules. And I believe that, after I don't know how many years, I shall succeed in convincing those in authority that it will be safe to let me return to society and that I can still be a useful member of it."

"Charles Newcomb will never be given a full pardon by me," said Governor Ernest Lister.

On August 1, 1920, while Newcomb was umpiring a prison baseball game, fellow inmate Charles "Black Diamond" Wilson hit him over the head, killing him. The blow was the result of a ruling between rival prison teams.

Chapter 18

INTRODUCING
AMANDA TRUELOVE

Ask any local historian who Tacoma's most famous madam was, and the answer will invariably be Lillian "Amanda Truelove" Buckley. She arrived in town sometime after 1915 and set up shop using various last names—Cox, Coyne and McClure, as well as Buckley and Truelove—which makes researching her difficult. Was she the Amanda Truelove who was granted a pauper's allowance in 1908 in Mississippi? It's possible, but there were many Trueloves all over the South. Was she related to Tom Truelove, a "negro" who, in 1909, pleaded guilty to the charge of stealing and selling a saddle in New Mexico? Maybe. She was Black. Was she the Amanda Cox who in October 1914 filed for divorce from Joseph B. Cox in Idaho, asking for half of their $30,000 community property? Who's to say? All these fit her. What we do know for sure is that while living in Salt Lake City and going by the name Amanda Truelove McClure, she killed her husband, Samuel McClure.

She was born in 1889 in Denton, Texas, and was twenty-six years old when she shot her thirty-three-year-old spouse through the head in the bathroom at their home (or "his" home, as the newspaper said) at 433 West Forth Street—less than five weeks after their May 4 marriage.

"A friend of my husband's, Bob Mason, brought his [her husband's] mail to him at the house about noon," Truelove-McClure told the police. "And I noticed one letter from Memphis in a woman's handwriting. When he opened it, I snatched it away from him and saw that she had addressed him

Amanda Truelove's mugshot. *Public domain.*

as 'my dear husband.' He afterwards admitted that he had another wife and told me that he would kill me if I made any trouble about it." She went on to say that his bigamy was a complete surprise. Because of that and his treatment of her, she bought a revolver to protect herself. On June 8, she shot him during a family quarrel.

Truelove-McClure was officially charged in June, but one of the witnesses went missing. When arraignment resumed on August 13, she pleaded not guilty, claiming the shooting was in self-defense. Testifying on behalf of the state were Patrolman N.P. Pierce, Dr. Hardie Lynch and W.R. Davidson, an occupant of the house where the shooting occurred. Her trial began on September 23, the prosecution rested on October 1 and her defense began the next day, resting on October 4. On October 15, after only an hour's deliberations, the jury found her not guilty. From then until mid-November 1923, Amanda Truelove-McClure was off the radar.

On November 17, 1923, under the name Lillian Buckley (who gave her age as twenty-eight instead of thirty-four), she and E.T Hartley, operator of a soft drink parlor, were charged with the murder of Clarence W. Woodard, a Spanish-American War veteran and recently discharged Camp Lewis soldier. Deputy prosecuting attorney Leo Teats investigated the death, which occurred at the Superior Hotel, 1313½ Broadway, taking into consideration a statement given by another former soldier, Mitchell Silk.

According to Silk, he and forty-nine-year-old Woodard—who had enlisted in the Wisconsin Volunteers in 1898, at the outbreak of the Spanish-American War, and had subsequently served in "various enlistments in the regular army"—had begun visiting saloons to celebrate Woodard's discharge from Camp Lewis, using the veteran's discharge money: $244.55. The last place they hit was the Edmonds Hotel at 1333 Pacific Avenue, where Hartley and Buckley served them. "During the drinking," Silk said, "Buckley brought over 'an alcoholic concoction which she told them had been prepared officially for Woodard.'" Shortly after he drank it, the former soldier became unconscious. Silk said that's when he saw Buckley take Woodard's wallet out of his pocket. She then gave Silk $45 and asked him to take his friend out of the establishment. Once outside, Silk hailed a vehicle and had his companion taken to the Superior Hotel. Woodard died, and Buckley and Hartley were arrested and charged with murder. Silk was also arrested but on other charges. Following the coroner's report, Teats said the drink probably contained wood alcohol.

On December 1, 1923, Tacoma officials set a trial for the pair to begin on January 8. They were accused of giving the discharged soldier "a poison drink in order to stupefy and then rob him." In February, Buckley was released after presenting a bond. In March, she was sentenced to from three to fifteen years for grand larceny but was acquitted on a first-degree murder charge. She was retried the following year, and on January 15, 1925, a hung jury failed to convict either of them.

For eight years she was, again, off the radar.

We next find the purveyor of illegal alcohol with the name Amanda Truelove Coyne, wife of George Coyne, who was arrested in October 1933 on a charge of murder. Coyne was a thirty-nine-year-old former army sergeant who ran a Tacoma rooming house at 1545 Market Street and had a ranch on the border of Pierce and King Counties. It was destroyed by a fire that killed sisters Jean Kanzler, age seven, and Gloria, age six; their mother, Vera Stone; and their stepfather, Arthur Stone, caretakers of the ranch.

On the night of the fire, which began at 12:30 a.m., Coyne told authorities he'd been drinking heavily and that the smoke woke him up; he also said his pants caught fire and the pain woke him. Whether it was the smoke or the pain, he escaped from the burning building and went to a nearby hill, where he laid down and fell asleep. He said he left the inferno because he couldn't stand hearing the cries of the "burning people."

An investigation revealed that Coyne's shirt and shoes had blood on them. He said it could have come from a cut or from a fight he'd had a month previously or from his trying to rescue the children. Coyne's *que sera sera* attitude sent prosecutor Robert M. Burgunder and deputy prosecutor William J. Wilkins to the scene of the fire. They and Deputy Sheriffs R.A.J. Allingham and William H. Sears uncovered a partially burned blanket, an axe, a crowbar, a rifle and a kerosene jug.

An inquest was held, and Betty Inge, a former resident of Coyne's Tacoma rooming house, testified that he had threatened to blow up both the ranch house and the rooming house. His threats caused her to move to Seattle. Two of Coyne's other rooming house tenants, Cornelia Cornio and Elizabeth Hall, corroborated Inge's statements, saying Coyne threatened several times to destroy the property rather than lose it. He was involved in litigation pertaining to two different loans, one of $1,650 and the other of $800 made by a loan company to his wife. In his lawsuit, the defendant asked that the contracts be set aside due to the exorbitant interest rates being charged. However, when the contract for the larger loan was set aside in Superior Court, the decision was appealed to the Supreme Court.

Inge also said Coyne and his wife quarreled over the Stones, whom Amanda Truelove Coyne wanted to keep on at the ranch as caretakers but whom George wanted replaced. He slapped his wife and, according to Inge, said he intended to divorce her as soon as a property settlement could be made. Nevertheless, while he was in jail, Coyne was called the "Candy Kid" because of his weakness for bonbons and chocolate supplied by his wife during her many visits, in spite of their contentious relationship.

On October 16, a tentative jury was approved. Although those involved in the fire were Tacoma residents, the trial was held in Seattle because the farmhouse was several hundred feet north of the Pierce/King boundary line. Once deliberations began, a clerk at the Selden Law Office testified to having witnessed the two Coynes arguing over a $2,500 loan. The clerk said Coyne became very angry and walked out in the middle of the discussion. Nor was his wife with him in the courtroom. Instead, Coyne's mother sat next to him. The reason given was that Coyne was white, and his wife's race was thought to be an issue. The defense attorney said his client wasn't getting a fair trial because Mrs. Coyne was "a negress." The judge told the jury to disregard her race; the defense contended that her "race was brought in by the State to prejudice the jury." Whether it was due to her race or the contentious husband-wife relationship, she was absent from the courtroom.

Coyne's trial lasted only a week. The evidence against him included the above-mentioned axe, crowbar, blanket, rifle and kerosene jug found at the scene and the bloodstains on his clothes. Investigations of the bodies showed that both Mr. and Mrs. Stone had been injured prior to the fire and that both children had fractured skulls. The prosecutor wanted to know why, although Coyne said he heard the children screaming and said he'd tried to save them, their remains indicated they hadn't moved from their beds; why, if Coyne had had as much to drink as he claimed, he was the first to wake when smoke and flames filled the house; and why the only thing he managed to save was a jug of whiskey.

A man named Bernard Kofoed also spoke for the prosecution. He said he and George Robbins were driving home from a dance when a man who appeared to be dazed came over a hill and sat on a log near the smoldering ruins and told them about his escape from the house. The man was Coyne, and he asked the pair to help him get out of King County. Kofoed started driving him toward Tacoma but made their passenger get out of the car after a fight began.

Irene Guy, who lived near the farm, said the fire must have started quickly. When she drove past the property, there was no fire, but on her return trip a few minutes later, smoke and flames were shooting into the air.

And when Deputy Sheriff Harry Pole testified, he said Mrs. Coyne had accompanied her husband to the scene of the fire, where he said to her, "Lil, keep your damn mouth shut, I'll do all the talking here."

Other people gave evidence; the trouble was, their comments were mostly hearsay. Coyne's attorney had asked for "a directed verdict of not guilty," saying the state was unable to provide a motive. Ignoring the victims' bodily injuries, he said, "There was no evidence that the victims had been killed by violence, and no proof that the fire was arson."

The judge said, "The secret of what happened is locked in that house, and it will never be known." He also called Coyne a drunken, cowardly scoundrel.

On October 25, for the first time since his June 22 arrest, George Coyne was home. And back at the Tacoma rooming house, Amanda Truelove McClure Coyne was out of his life and out of the picture. But she would be back.

Approximately four months after the death of his children, their father, Fred Kanzler, hanged himself in his Tacoma home on February 12, 1934.

In the 1920s, Tacoma was a fast-growing town that suffered from a split personality. Buildings were going up all over. On Pacific Avenue, for

The Coffee Pot Restaurant (Java Jive). *Courtesy of the Library of Congress.*

example, those being built included the National Bank of Tacoma in 1921, Brotherhood Cooperative National Bank in 1924 and the Bank of California in 1928. The fifteen-story Washington Building, home to the Brotherhood Cooperative, with its high-speed elevators, was the second-tallest building in the Pacific Northwest. Just down the street, the North Coast Stage Lines/ Central Bus Terminal began operating in 1929. Tacoma's First Sears and Roebuck store was at 2314–24 Pacific Avenue, with Cunningham Electric Company as an across-the-street neighbor. Other businesses included the Coffee Pot Restaurant, now known as the Java Jive. It was built in sections on the tide flats and then bolted together on site, becoming one of Tacoma's first prefabricated commercial buildings. Its neighbor was the nationally known Roman Meal Company, currently one of four companies operating under Dakota Specialty Enterprises. The cornerstone was laid for Bellarmine College for Boys, and on Proctor Street, a new Paramount Theater opened. Unfortunately, these achievements were balanced with all that was wicked about the town.

Chapter 19

THE FIRST MAJOR KIDNAPPING

Arthur Rust

On February 1, 1921, twenty-year-old Arthur Rust, son of banker, real estate owner and mining and smelting man W.R. Rust (he of the smelter and the Rust Home on North Twenty-First Street), was kidnapped and his father sent a ransom note asking for $25,000.

At the time of the kidnapping, W.R. Rust had sold the Twenty-First Street mansion, and the family was living at 512 North Yakima. Arthur was walking to his job at the Union Bank of California when a car pulled up near the corner of Division Street and Broadway. The driver, who wore a leather coat and helmet, asked the young man if he wanted a ride, which he did. However, once he was in the car, the man tied a blanket around Arthur's head and upper body. At the corner nearest the bank, the driver drew a pistol and said, "Keep quiet if you value your life."

He drove to the Puget Sound Iron and Steel Works garage on the tide flats and forced Rust to write the ransom note, which also said that if the money wasn't forthcoming, he "would be found dead." Then he left the young man in the building and took off. Though the police didn't think he had anything to do with the crime, officers arrested a messenger boy named Robert Berg, age twenty-three, who delivered the note to Rust's father.

Down on the tide flats, Arthur managed to free himself from the blanket and rope and asked a Black man for help. A superintendent from a nearby factory came to assist. Someone called both W.R. Rust and the police.

Arthur Rust. *Courtesy of Find a Grave.*

But when the cops arrived, the kidnapper, of course, was gone; however, Arthur said he could identify his assailant.

A $500 reward was offered, and on March 8, a former marine, twenty-three-year-old Hugh C. Van Amburgh, was arrested. All should have gone well—but it didn't. First, Van Amburgh was a World War I hero. He had served with the famed Second Division in France, had been awarded two Croix de Guerre and received a Distinguished Service Cross, which the president noted was "for extraordinary heroism while serving with the Headquarters Company, Fourth Brigade [marines], 2d Division, A.E.F., in action near Vierzy, France, 19 July 1918. As a motorcycle dispatch rider, Corporal Van Amburgh made repeated trips along shell-swept roads and in a gassed area, before and during the capture of Vierzy. When Vierzy was still in German hands, he dismounted from his motorcycle in front of the town and, with great coolness and disregard of personal safety, snuck in and brought back information of great value to his brigade commander."

Tacoma tidelands, circa 1910. *Courtesy of the Library of Congress.*

Unfortunately, Van Amburgh's brother said, the former veteran was "suffering from the effects of the war and had become unbalanced." And second, while taking the stand in spite of his PTSD, Van Amburgh testified that Arthur Rust had plotted the kidnapping in order to get money out of his father.

To a packed courtroom, Van Amburgh said, "Arthur Rust told me he needed money. He was loath to ask his father for the sum required, and asked if I would like to make a big sum easily. I told him yes. He then said his father was afraid of kidnappers and he suggested a kidnapping plot. I told him," Van Amburgh went on to say, that "it was a dirty trick. He answered that all the Rust wealth would be his someday and getting a little in advance made no difference."

On the stand, W.R. said when he'd received the note, he immediately withdrew the money from the bank and headed for the designated drop-off spot but couldn't find it. He then returned to his office and learned that his son was free.

Calling two witnesses, attorney M.J. Gordon attempted to show that Arthur Rust and his client were well acquainted, something Arthur Rust denied.

Judge W.D. Askren allowed Van Amburgh's war record to be taken into consideration when rendering a verdict; defense attorneys protested. Gordon planned to subpoena more than a dozen witnesses, but they were probably never called. After only four hours of deliberations, Van Amburgh was acquitted. He later repudiated his signed statement of collusion with Rust.

TIDE LANDS.

Hugh Clifford Van Amburgh died on January 23, 1939, in Portland, Oregon. He was only forty. His postwar jobs included going into the machinery business with his father; operating a garage in Longview, Washington; working for Standard Oil Company and the Goodrich Tire Company; and running a café in Portland. He left a wife and son.

Whether or not Arthur Rust was guilty has always been up for debate. Sadly, his reputation was still tarnished when he died from heart problems on May 13, 1936.

Part IV

....

DEPRESSION-ERA ECONOMICS

Chapter 20

ORGANIZED CRIME IN TACOMA?

Tacoma for more than two years has rubbed elbows with the most despicable criminals in America without knowing it. This city now learns that it has become a national "cooling off spot" for major mobsters. Following the killing of F.B.I. Special Agent W. Carter Baum during the Dillinger gun battle at Little Bohemia Lodge, Wisconsin, George "Baby Face" Nelson hid out there for a time while seeking to escape the guns of avenging government men.
Albert Bates, kidnapping partner of George "Machine Gun" Kelly was also a temporary Tacoman during his free days, and was once a star roomer at a highly respectable home here [Tacoma] *which took in "gentlemen residents," and that his constant companion was a machine gun with which he guarded the stairway in case of a police attack. Likewise, the names of notorious killers, bank robbers, bunco and confidence men from San Francisco and Reno are mentioned casually in the underworld. Thus, the whole city suddenly has become heavily affected with the jitters.*
—Seattle Post-Intelligencer, *June 1, 1935*

In February 1923, when the newspapers printed lists of approved building permits, Tacoma residents read that a man named Robert McKinnell was having a Paramount movie theater built at 3816 North Twenty-Sixth Street just off Procter Street. As always in those days, construction was quick. When the theater opened four months later, the *Tacoma Daily Ledger* described its façade as being of "tastefully designed geometric patterns created using alternating brown and white pressed bricks. Outside, four columns, two on each side of the entry, are made from white bricks which are bordered with brown ones. The front has a window on each side of the door and one above it. Inside is a proscenium [the arch separating the stage from the auditorium] and on each side of the arch are oil paintings on silk, one of Mt. Rainier and one of Snoqualmie Falls, both lit from behind."

The movie house opened on June 10, 1923, with a Photoplay organ accompanying the movie *Back Home and Broke*.

While McKinnell was busy running the theater, gangster Frank Nitti of Chicago and his New York cohort, Lucky Luciano, were making plans to take over Hollywood. Nitti in particular wanted to control the movie studios because they seemed to him to be never-ending sources of money and because he thought movie stars were gullible drunks, drug addicts and big spenders. Nitti put "mob-controlled union leader George Browne" in charge, and Browne teamed up with Willie Bioff, a Chicago pimp and racketeer and "labor leader in the movie production business." Whatever money they collected would be laundered through Al Capone's soup kitchens.

Nitti was also interested in the projectionists' union and began by going after Balaban and Katz, the B&K Theater chain. Unless B&K paid $20,000, every projectionist was to be pulled off his job. To make his point, some of Browne's soldiers burned down several B&K theaters. However, Browne and Bioff didn't always burn the movie houses; sometimes they smoked them out. A soldier would ignite the end of a reel of nitrate film, which was rolled so tight that instead of burning, it sent pungent smoke and toxic fumes into the auditorium. When this happened, patrons fled, the theater was shut down, health department officials had to inspect the premises and owners lost business. On December 30, 1930, a smoke bomb went off at Robert McKinnell's Twenty-Sixth and Proctor Street Paramount Theater. Employees who found the source of the problem said it was "skunk essence with perhaps a dash of gas." They also said they'd seen a man leave the seat where the bomb was found a few seconds before the odoriferous event began.

The fumes quickly dissipated, and only one person was too ill to go back inside. While a friend walked her home, the other 198 people returned to see the end of the film.

Whether or not the theater was a Nitti target, one federal investigator wrote that "Tacoma was under the dominance of an Italian Super Government with a prominent bootlegger as its director."

A federal investigation cited thirty-seven brothels and bootlegging joints within eleven blocks of city hall.

Chapter 21

VITO CUTTONE AND HIS ITALIAN MAFIA

Vito Cuttone was born on May 31, 1892, in Campobello, Italy, to Joseppe and Angela Stallon Cuttone. There is no record that they ever immigrated, but in June 1917, Cuttone was living in Tacoma, hoping to make a living as a tailor. He advertised for a coat maker, giving his address as 504 South Eleventh Street. He either lived or worked there (or perhaps both). The address would put him just below Tacoma Avenue South, between Fawcett Street and Court E. The 1920 census has him living with twenty-five-year-old Burt Mange and Gonny Tigano and Domenico Canale, both thirty. The 1930 census, however, shows that Cuttone was married to a Canadian woman named Marjorie and was working as a distributor for the Auburn Automobile Company as president of the Tacoma branch. Writing about the business, a newspaper article said Cuttone "contributes to the organization a vast business experience in many branches of merchandise."

The company was founded in 1900 in Auburn, Indiana, and was moderately successful until materials shortages during World War I forced its closure. The plant was sold twice, but eventually, the Depression along with the automobile's high cost became a bad combination. By 1937, the Auburn was defunct. Also by that time, Cuttone had other interests. Back in 1926, Cuttone had been identified by federal authorities as Tacoma's most powerful bootlegger along with his "chief lieutenant," a man named Frank Magrini. According to a man named Edward Heinemann, "finding horses for Washington owners started with an Italian fellow in Tacoma named Frank Magrini. He loved the races and had a few cheap mares."

"Horses" aside, the Treasury Department said the two were linked to "an Italian Super-Government that controlled Tacoma's police department and city hall." On January 15, 1935, Cuttone, Primo Rosellini and a third man, most likely Mike Vendetti, were indicted by a grand jury, charged with collecting protection money.

In a letter from L. Dene Hickman, agent in charge, to W.E. Kain, special agent of the Bureau of Prohibition, Hickman wrote:

On May 3, 1932, a large seizure of alcohol was made at Tacoma by Sheriff Freemont Campbell and investigation has disclosed that this alcohol was shipped by box car to Vito Cuttone, who has been the bigshot in Tacoma for some time. It was found that Cuttone was seen about Tacoma during the last ten days with a Jew from Cleveland, Ohio who he was introducing to various characters in the local underworld and it is reported that this Jew showed a printed price list about Tacoma giving wholesale prices of bonded liquor and alcohol to be shipped from Cleveland, Ohio and he occupied a room at the Winthrop Hotel for about ten days. This man is now at the New Heathman Hotel in your city and will remain there until about May 10th when he goes to San Francisco, California and will stop at the Palace Hotel there. He is reported to look a great deal like Special Agent Close with whom you are acquainted, is about five feet, six inches tall, dark complexion, well dressed and weighs about 140 pounds. This information is being sent to you with the possibility that a surveillance of this man's activities while in Portland, and a check of whom he meets might lead to a similar transaction in Portland as was completed in Tacoma. Mr. Amster is believed to be the solicitor for a large liquor combine in the east, and it is very probable that the seizure in Tacoma will be investigated by the Special Agents, any information you might secure at Portland will very probably fit into the case in good shape.

As with Cuttone, there are few newspaper articles about either Rosellini or Vendetti. According to the 1940 census, Rosellini was born in 1886 (his grave marker says 1885) in Italy, his wife's name was Cesarina and they had two children. He was an associate of Charles Romeo and John Rosellini, a cousin, both arrested in late January 1927 and convicted of violating the federal narcotics act, having in their possession between $60,000 and

$100,000 worth of morphine and cocaine. They were doing time on McNeil Island when, in February 1928, Primo and John's cousin Frank was found guilty of thirteen counts of liquor violation.

When it comes to tracking down Cuttone, however, he was even more elusive than Amanda Truelove. Sam Angeloff, a *Seattle Post-Intelligencer* staff writer, once said, "His name figured more in Tacoma's political history than that of most any other man. Yet he held no office. His name figured in more news-making events in coffee table talk and yet he was rarely mentioned in the newspapers."

During Prohibition, Tacoma was like other parts of the country in that our Italian mob reached the heights of its power, figuring prominently in the distribution of bootlegged and smuggled liquor. According to Eric Timothy's book *More Than a Century of Service: The History of the Tacoma Police Department*:

> *Documents from the Department of Justice and the Bureau of Prohibition, included Amster, debt-collector Mike Vendetti, the "negro gambler" Pat Wright, and Wright's brothel-owning brother, nicknamed "Fish House," who was forced to leave town when he was unable to produce $200 in protection money for Vendetti. This colorful cast of characters was the focus of a six year federal investigation.*

Available government records offer few details about the outcome of the investigation. In response to my request to the Federal Bureau of Investigation for Freedom of Information documents from 1920 to 1940, I was told, "We conducted a search of the places reasonably expected to have records. However, we were unable to identify records responsive to your request." And a rather poorly written draft of a document in a local newspaper reads as follows:

> *A thousand pieces and no sneers of dying lords of the former lords of the ring can change or destroy the mass of data now being whipped into the form of evidence to put the seal of doom on those who in the years past have sat in the lap of criminal luxury and laughed at the futile efforts of local authorities to prevent it.*

There is no doubt that Washington State's early ban on alcohol "facilitated the distribution of liquor that was either manufactured by local bootleggers or smuggled in from Canada by 'rum runners' who delivered their goods to secret waterfront locations under cover of night. Not surprisingly, a number of police officers and city officials quickly learned that good money could be made protecting (or at least ignoring) these illicit dealings."

The Bureau of Prohibition began investigating Cuttone and his cohorts in 1926 and continued until 1932. On August 6, 1926, Vendetti was tried before the Ninth Circuit Court on "a charge of conspiracy entered into on or about November 28, 1925, to unlawfully possess and sell intoxicating liquors, and to unlawfully conduct and maintain a common nuisance at 1303 Pacific Avenue, Tacoma, Wash., by there keeping and selling intoxicating liquors, which conspiracy was alleged to be a continuing one from November 28, 1925, to June 3, 1926, and the indictment set forth numerous overt acts done in pursuance of the conspiracy."

Part of the evidence was that

> on January 13, 1926, two government officers bought drinks of moonshine whisky in the restaurant, and that on January 27, 1926, they bought drinks from Moore (charges against him were dropped); that at that time the defendant was seen there talking with Nelson (his charges were also dropped) behind the bar; that on February 17, 1926, the officers bought Scotch whisky at the same place, and saw other customers being served with intoxicating liquor, and that Nelson and Moore were attending the bar; that on February 23, 1926, the officers were again at the premises and saw the defendant sitting there talking with Nelson, and that in the defendant's presence they each bought a half pint of moonshine whisky; that on June 3, 1926, one of the officers bought a drink of moonshine whisky from Carstens (again, charges dropped); that on February 23, 1926, when an officer asked the defendant if they could get something to drink, and "if they were closing up," he replied, "No, you can get something to drink."

After the indictment, Mike Vendetti disappeared.

According to the website tacomaprohibitiontales.wordpress.com, when the heat was on, "Cuttone either left town, served time, or escaped punishment." But hustling liquor during Prohibition was easy. The Beach Tavern on Sixth Avenue near Titlow regularly received shipments of whiskey, rum, beer and illegal Chinese immigrants. "Slavs" drank at "clubs" near the north end of Pearl Street; Italians frequented the Toscano Café at Fifteenth and Broadway, which was raided in 1926, 1931 and 1946; and University of Puget Sound students were all too familiar with the still at 2121 North Union Street.

When the "dry squad" was out, no one was safe. Stills were uncovered at 3611 South Thirty-First, 916 South Third, 6016 South Tyler, 2806 South A Street, 503 South Thirtieth and 5413 South Washington, among many other places. The worst female offender was said to be Theresa Torchini, who was arrested thirty times, had twelve police convictions and two run-ins with federal agents and got out of her last charge only because Prohibition was repealed. The illegal liquor business was too lucrative for Cuttone to stay away for long, and as long as Prohibition remained in effect, Puget Sound waterways made bootlegging easy.

In 1932, a syndicate of "racketeers ran the city from bottom to top." At least three dozen brothels fueled by illegal liquor operated openly within eleven blocks of city hall, according to records from the U.S. Treasury Department, which then included the Bureau of Prohibition. Every joint paid monthly protection fees. Gangsters greased city leaders with the proceeds in exchange for police indifference. Police Commissioner Dyer Dyment got a cut. So did Police Chief Marvin Guy. Mayor Melvin G. Tennant commanded the biggest payoff: $1,000 a month, federal records say. Even federal liquor agents were on the take, according to the old records.

Vito Cuttone, described as "a seemingly mild-mannered car dealer with an inscrutable smile and a knack for persuasion," ran the syndicate and was the "chief fixer, king bootlegger, collector, ruling head, self-styled cousin of Al Capone." Sean Robinson of the *News Tribune* wrote, "With Dyment, Guy and Tennant on his personal payroll, Cuttone controlled department assignments, ensuring free rein for the speakeasies and brothels under his protection, federal agents found." When a waitress named Grace Stonequist was murdered, investigators considered "Cuttone's syndicate and the public officials under his control" as the culprits. More than twenty years later, when police officers tried to reopen the case, all the files were missing.

A three-man police "dry squad" oversaw vice, liquor and prostitution enforcement. The agents interviewed beat cops, who said they were instructed not to interfere with the squad. Any officer who broke ranks and dinged a protected joint could expect swift reassignment, sometimes within hours, typically to a night shift in "the sticks."

Washington made all forms of gambling illegal in 1889. In 1893, Gustav Friedrich Wilhelm Schultze's "horseshoe slot machine" was the first of its type to include an automatic payout mechanism. Two years later, Charles Fey invented a modified version of the horseshoe that paid out coins; this machine became incredibly popular. In 1940, not long after the Volstead Act was repealed, Cuttone bought Sandberg's old place, rebuilt it and

Confiscated bootlegging paraphernalia. *Courtesy of the Library of Congress.*

opened the four-hundred-seat Cameo Theater. The theater's inaugural motion picture, *Hard Guy*, starred Jack La Rue as a racketeer who ran a nightclub where the working girls married the rich blueblood customers and then blackmailed them into annulments and cash settlements. Cuttone also ran a protection racket for a variety of illegal operations, including renting out pinball machines, which, because of his connections with the police, encouraged some officers and their bosses to look the other way. Tacoma historian Michael Sullivan gave this example: "Monthly rent for one pinball machine: $100; monthly payoff to Cuttone: $300. For that money, Cuttone's people would come by and make sure the cops did not break you up."

By 1960, the City of Tacoma owned the abandoned Cameo Theater building. It was torn down, and an Escalade was built between Pacific Avenue and Commerce Street. As the nation's first moving sidewalk, it won Tacoma a national award for urban progress. "Urban progress" notwithstanding, it was eventually shut down. Then in 1968, when local architect Bob Evans investigated redeveloping the Escalade, he stumbled into a Turkish bath, beautifully preserved, having been closed for so many years.

Chapter 22

WHEN BANK ROBBING WAS A PRIORITY

Ed Bentz

Send me to Alcatraz; all my friends are there.
—Ed Bentz

He was an avid reader who liked to live among scholarly people; he preferred peace and quiet, art and good companions; he owned several volumes of rare books, visited used bookstores in the cities he traveled through; collected rare coins and corresponded with other numismatics; he liked golf, nightclubbing and dancing; and in his book, *Persons in Hiding*, J. Edgar Hoover called him "the shrewdest, most resourceful, intelligent and dangerous bank robber in existence."

Information about Ed Bentz's early life is scarce. He was born on June 2, 1894, in Pipestone, Minnesota, to German immigrants George and Rose Wall (or Wahl). But when Ed's father was killed by a runaway horse, his mother used the insurance money to move the family to Tacoma, where she owned a boardinghouse and operated a theater. Ed and his eight brothers and sisters had respectable childhoods, but Ed liked nothing better than stealing cigarettes and bicycles from his friends. In October 1909, he and a friend broke into Puyallup's Morris Mill feed house. The paper said, "Puyallup has been caused considerable trouble by a gang of 'little toughs'" and that Bentz had "been free from trouble until he fell into bad company." Nevertheless, Bentz became a guest of the Chehalis State Training School in 1910. He escaped and the following year was picked up at the Tacoma Fir Door Company plant and given from one to five years in the Monroe "reformatory." The year 1912 found him a resident at the Tacoma jail, arrested for stealing a car. He escaped, was picked up again and ended up at the Walla Wall penitentiary—apparently, not for long. After trying to pass a forged check for thirty-four dollars in a local department store, a judge sentenced him to from 18 months to 20 years. That was on December 12, 1916. Between his youth in Tacoma and his final arrest in 1936, Bentz "was sentenced to 34.5 years by various jurisdictions around the country" but only served 7 years. Early parole, release after serving minimum time, jumping bail and talking his way out of accusations all played their part.

Bentz slowly graduated from "unorganized crimes" to nighttime burglaries and breaking into post offices and banks, "cutting into safes with a 150-pound torch." The torch was heavy, and faster cars on better roads meant quick getaways from a daytime robbery. "I decided to become a yegg. A bank robber, you know," he told an FBI agent. "They're the aristocracy of the criminal profession."

Even as a rookie, Bentz knew the keys to success in his chosen profession were education and organization. He used his infrequent imprisonments to pick the brains of the "more seasoned prison mates." Bentz's theory was that robberies where guns have to be used were poorly planned, and he insisted his cohorts use them for intimidation only. When planning a job, he visited the local library to study documents "about a bank's assets and liabilities, and to determine how much cash would be in a bank" at any one time. He visited banks and posed as a possible investor or businessman who was thinking of opening an account. When doing so, he'd "wrangle" a guided tour and check out the security features. He limited his heists to three a year, "read everything he could dealing with law enforcement and regularly kept up with any changes in state and federal statutes." He learned that insurance companies would buy back "bonds at five, 10 or 15 cents on the dollar" and that negotiable bonds (probably bearer bonds, which are unregistered) and some securities "could be worth more than cash when sold." He knew how to launder bonds using overseas transactions. He later bragged that he had $1 million worth of bonds buried; he was waiting until the market cooled down and he could sell them. He was so knowledgeable that other gangsters asked for financial advice.

On September 17, 1930, Bentz organized and led the holdup of the Lincoln National Bank and Trust for "more than a million dollars in cash, bonds, and commercial paper ("a short-term debt instrument issued by companies to raise funds generally for a time period up to one year.... They are typically issued by large banks or corporations to cover short-term receivables and meet short-term financial obligations, such as funding for a new project."). A year later, almost to the day, the police got a tip and arrested him for a bank holdup in Madison, Indiana, and brought him in for questioning regarding a telephone company bond theft in Chicago. The following November, authorities in McKinney, Texas, picked him up for a robbery in nearby Blue Ridge.

After doing time in Walla Walla, Bentz had done some jobs but little time in Illinois and Missouri. In 1932, he teamed up with George "Machine Gun Kelly," robbing a bank in Ponder, Texas, on July 31; taking part in "a machine gun robbery" at the Bank of Colfax (in Washington) on September 21; and hitting a Holland, Michigan bank eight days later. He was picked up in Texas but jumped bond, escaped and moved to Long Beach, Indiana, planning to give life in semi-retirement a try.

But not for long.

The following year, Lester "Baby Face" Nelson asked Bentz to organize a heist. Bentz located a "good bank" in Grand Haven, Michigan, arranged for "Tommy guns, and a barrel of roofing nails to throw on the street and slow down pursuers" and was talked into participating. From a getaway driver who left the robbers in the bank and took off, to armed citizens firing at them, to hostages falling off the running boards of moving vehicles, to Baby Face getting off rounds of automatic fire, everything went wrong. Bentz escaped, stayed hot for the "first time in years" and moved to the Northeast, where he tried to go legit. It started with his brother Theodore, a fellow yegg.

One day while sitting on a Florida beach, Theodore said, "I'm tired of being on the lam all the time." He suggested they start a legitimate business up north someplace where no one would know them. They could incorporate, and Ed would be president. By April 1, 1934, they were living in an upscale neighborhood on Washington Avenue in Portland, Maine. On April 1, 1934, "corporation papers were drawn up to start Ultra Products, a company which manufactured and distributed small metal toys such as horses, elephants, and dogs, wrapped in cellophane to be sold in candy stores." The business was across St. John Street from Union Station, and Bentz, going by the name Frederick Wendell, went on the road to sell their products. He was "legit" for about four weeks. "Things aren't going right," he said. "I don't seem to be able to push this merchandise. Either I raise some new capital or Ultra Products goes broke."

And so, on June 4, he dressed as a farmer; strolled into a Danville, Vermont bank; and robbed it. The next day, he saw his picture on the front page of the *Boston Herald* with the caption "Wanted for Bank Robbery."

At this point in his life, the forty-year-old Bentz had a twenty-two-year-old wife named Verna. After seeing his picture in the paper, they left Portland and headed for New York. In the city, they moved once a month. With their "glamourous life of sparkle and excitement" gone, Verna was gone, too. She had her things shipped to her parents' home at 704 Monroe Street in South Milwaukee and followed them by train.

Never has Michigan seen a better organized crime syndicate...the best of sub-machine guns, high powered rifles, shotguns, pistols, ammunition, bullet proof vests, armored automobiles, and medical equipment for treating its wounded.

—Oscar G. Olander, Michigan state police commissioner

Seeing the activity at the Monroe Street home, it was obvious to the FBI that something was up. When Verna arrived, they arrested her. Verna had been known to harbor her husband, said action violating a federal statute. They took her into custody and for questioning on March 7, 1936. Verna was probably telling the truth when she said she didn't know where her husband was, but when she innocently mentioned their having lived in a six-story apartment at 1492 Bushwick Avenue in Brooklyn, she sealed her husband's fate. Six days later, agents flooded the apartment with "teargas bombs and grenades" and arrested Bentz. They found him in a dumbwaiter, clinging to the ropes between the second and third floors while trying to reach the roof. He was wearing only his underwear.

At first, Bentz only confessed to robberies in Caledonia, Wisconsin, and Grand Haven, Michigan. Eventually, he confessed to six more but refused to name his accomplices. The known list included:

Theodore Bentz, who served life in the Marquette Branch Prison at Marquette, Michigan;
George "Baby Face" Nelson, killed by federal agents in a gunfight;
Tommy Carroll, killed in a gunfight with St. Paul police;
Freddie, "a mystery yegg." During the robbery of the People's Savings Bank of Grand Haven, he was the "nervous getaway car driver frightened off by local undertaker Edward D. Kinkema's sawed-off, automatic shotgun";
Homer Wilson, who died of natural causes;
Charles J. Fitzgerald, who was sent to Alcatraz, where he became one of the oldest prisoners there;
Campbell, first name unknown, killed by rival gangsters at Red Wing, Minnesota. According to medium.com, "In the early 1930s, Minnesota was

a haven for gangsters—infamous criminals such as John Dillinger, Alvin Karpis and Edna Murray;"

James L. Ripley, held as an accomplice in the Danville robbery;

Earl Doyle, accomplice of Eddie Green in robbing a bank messenger in North Kansas City, sentenced to life in Marquette Prison;

Eddie Doll, real name Edward Larue, member of Theodore "Handsome Jack" Klutas's College Kidnappers, a group of alumni from the University of Illinois who specialized in kidnapping wealthy mobsters for ransom. He was sent to Leavenworth, convicted of violating the Dyer Act, also known as the National Motor Vehicle Theft Act;

Fred Goetz, associate of the Barker-Karpis gang, killed in a drive-by shooting; and

Lee Turner, convicted of tax evasion.

Eddie Bentz was paroled from Alcatraz in 1948 and immediately sent to Massachusetts to serve time there. Six years later, he went to a federal prison in Sandstone, Minnesota. He returned to Tacoma in 1967, living at 5411 South Thompson Street. He died of a heart attack on October 31, 1979. His death certificate gave "salesman" and "specialty advertising" as his occupation and business.

Chapter 23

THE SECOND MAJOR KIDNAPPING

George Weyerhaeuser

Regular school hours were carefully kept in 1935 when nine-year-old George Weyerhaeuser was kidnapped. But on May 24, the children at Lowell School were released early, and George walked to Annie Wright Seminary to meet his sister, Ann, and to connect with the family's chauffer, who would drive them home for lunch. With time on his hands, he arrived at the seminary ten or fifteen minutes ahead of the norm, and instead of waiting, he decided to walk back to his house along an overgrown path bordering the Tacoma Lawn Tennis Club. The tract ended at Borough Road, where two men were sitting in a 1927 Buick sedan. The passenger got out and approached George, asking for directions to Stadium Way. Then he grabbed the boy, hustled him into the back seat and covered him with an old blanket.

When George didn't return home, his family made a brief search before notifying the police. That evening, a mailman arrived with a special delivery letter addressed "To Whom It May Concern" with the boy's signature on it. The letter gave the family five days to raise a ransom of $200,000 in small, unmarked bills. It went on to say, "In five days or as soon as you have the money, advertise in the *Seattle P-I* personal column. Say 'We are ready.' And sign it Percy Minnie." The family would then be told where to deliver the ransom. Someone calling himself "Egoist" signed the message.

Following the 1932 kidnapping of Charles Lindbergh Jr., Congress adopted a federal kidnapping statute that let federal authorities step in and pursue kidnappers once they had taken their victims across state lines.

A young George Weyerhaeuser. *Courtesy of the Tacoma Public Library.*

George was the grandson of Friedrich Weyerhaeuser, the eighth-richest American of all time. Almost immediately, more than a dozen FBI agents arrived in Tacoma "to investigate leads."

Once the ransom money was collected—approximately twenty thousand bills—the agents made note of the serial numbers and sent a list to FBI headquarters in Washington, D.C., where they were recorded on a ten-page document. It was "for publication and distributed to post offices, banks, hotels, railway depots, and other commercial centers where money would change hands."

The day after George went missing, his family placed the following ads in the *Seattle Post-Intelligencer*'s personals column classified want ads. The first read: "Expect to be ready to come Monday. Answer. Percy Minnie." The second read: "Due to publicity beyond our control, please indicate another method of reaching you. Hurry, relieve anguished mother. Percy Minnie," and finally, "We are ready. Percy Minnie."

According to historylink.org, "The ransom negotiations were kept secret; the press received no further information. Law enforcement authorities agreed to refrain from any interference until the boy was released."

Five days after George's abduction, the kidnappers contacted Mr. Weyerhaeuser, telling him to go to Seattle's Ambassador Hotel at 806 Union Street, register as James Paul Jones and wait for additional instructions. The missive included a handwritten note from George saying he was safe. His father did as instructed, and at 9:45 p.m. that evening, he received another note telling him to drive to South Renton Avenue and Sixty-Second Avenue South in Rainier Valley with the money and to look on the right side of the road for a stake with a white cloth. Weyerhaeuser found the stake with the cloth, and underneath was a note in a tin can telling him to drive straight ahead seven hundred feet to another white cloth and park with the lights on and the engine running. He did and waited three hours, but nothing happened, so he returned to Seattle.

Midmorning on Thursday, May 30, 1935, Weyerhaeuser received an anonymous telephone call asking why he had failed to follow the instructions in the second note. He said he had followed them. He was then advised he'd get new instructions "and it would be the last chance to save his son." That night, he received a telephone call from a man "affecting a European accent" who told him to drive with the money to 1105 East Madison Street and "look for a tin can, directly inside the gate on the right hand side, containing a note with further instructions." The new instructions told him to drive to the Half-Way House near Angle Lake on Pacific Highway (Old 99) and turn onto a specified side road. From there, he was to follow a string of tin cans each with a white flag and each containing a note. The last note told him where to park the car and to place the bag containing the $200,000 ransom on the front seat; leave the vehicle with the engine running, the dome light on and the driver's door open; and then walk down the road toward the highway. If the money was in order, George would be released within thirty hours. Weyerhaeuser did as instructed, and after walking what he said was about one hundred yards down the road, he heard noises and saw someone run from the underbrush, enter his car (a black 1933 Pontiac sedan) and drive away. Once on the highway, the anguished father caught a ride to Tacoma to await word.

Meanwhile, during the time his dad was raising money and driving around, George's abductors drove him around, "during which time he heard them whispering back and forth." Eventually, they stopped the car, removed the blanket and gave him an envelope on which to write his name. After that, the boy was blindfolded and carried across what he thought was a rushing stream. On the other side, they set him down and took his hand, and everyone walked on a narrow, uneven path through brush and trees for what George later estimated to be one-half to three-quarters of a mile to a hole approximately four square feet near a sizeable log. They put him in the hole, chained his right wrist and leg, removed the blindfold and covered the hole with a board, taking turns guarding it. But after a while, they began worrying that the police might find the hole. So, they carried George back to the car, put him in the trunk and drove for an hour to a new location. Once again, they walked through some woods, but this time they had to dig the hole for George. And this time, he had a seat from the car and two blankets to help make him more comfortable, and the hole was covered with tarpaper.

Investigators later determined that the two men and a woman drove through Washington and into Idaho and that once through Blanchard, Idaho, they followed the highway, eventually turning near a mountain. On May 31, they took George to a house and put him in a large closet with a mattress, two chairs and a small white table. That evening, they told him they were all leaving. On the way out, George saw a watch on the table indicating it was 5:55 p.m.

Then, it was back to the trunk for George while they drove to a shack near Issaquah. At about 3:30 a.m., his captors left him with two dirty blankets and a dollar stuffed in his pocket, saying to wait in the shack for his father, who would come to take him home. George was having none of that; he started walking down the road. Six miles later, he wandered onto Louis P. Bonifas's farm and announced his identity. The family took him in, and Willena Bonifas gave him breakfast and some dry shoes and socks. Then they piled into the family's Model T Ford and headed for Tacoma, making one stop—at a Union 76 to ask the attendant, Ernie Backlund, to call the boy's home. No one answered, so Mr. Bonifas called the Tacoma Police Department to let them know George was safe and that they were bringing him in.

Meanwhile, the FBI had been working on the case, taking precautions to ensure George's safe return. Immediately after the ransom was delivered, lists of the serial numbers were sent to all of the "Bureau's field offices for distribution to commercial enterprises, including banks, hotels and railway companies." On June 2, 1935, a twenty-dollar ransom bill was used to buy a railway ticket from Huntington, Oregon, to Salt Lake City, Utah. Agents determined the purchaser to be Harmon Metz Waley.

Shortly after that, more of the bills appeared in Salt Lake City discount stores. The number of special agents available there was limited, so police officers were placed in each downtown discount store, and each store was furnished a copy of the ten-page list of serial numbers. Their actions paid off; on June 8, a Woolworth cashier told the detective stationed there that a woman was trying to use one of the bills. The detective took the woman—Margaret E. Waley, Harmon's wife—to the FBI's Salt Lake City field office, where another ransom bill was discovered in her pocketbook. While she was telling conflicting stories, they got her address, and later that day, they arrested Harmon Waley at home. He told a number of lies before confessing that he and William Dainard, alias William Mahan, whom he had met in the Idaho State Penitentiary, had kidnapped the boy. He added that his wife had no knowledge of the kidnapping until their arrival in Spokane, Washington. She had, though, been at the hideout house and helped them negotiate the ransom. Waley said he and Dainard planned to split the money evenly but that Dainard cheated him out of $5,000. He also said he bought a Ford Roadster and, when he reached Salt Lake City, registered it using the name Herman Von Metz.

For some unknown reason, approximately $3,700 of the ransom money had been partially burned in the Waleys' stove. The remaining fragments were sent to an FBI laboratory in Washington, D.C., for examination. It was determined that enough of the numbers remained on the scraps of paper to make a positive identification. Physical evidence taken from the hideout, holes and kidnappers' homes, and especially the tin cans, unquestionably linked the Waleys and Dainard to the shack where the ransom had been divided.

On June 11, agents found $90,790 under a clump of trees and $15,500 in Dainard's abandoned car. Learning that Waley planned to connect with Dainard at the home of Margaret Waley's parents, agents also went there. Her grandfather told them that a man answering Dainard's description had come to the house looking for the Waleys. He had, he said, told the man that the Waleys had been there earlier to pick up their suitcase but that they returned to Salt Lake City and had been arrested. Hearing that, Dainard headed for Butte, Montana. An identification order, which included Dainard's photograph, fingerprints, handwriting specimen and background information, was prepared, and copies were distributed throughout the United States.

In early 1936, bills with altered serial numbers began to surface in the western part of the country. The FBI laboratory's examination of these bills revealed the true serial numbers to be identical to those on some of the ransom bills. Banks were advised to be alert to any person presenting possibly altered currency for exchange.

"On May 6, 1936, employees of two different Los Angeles, California banks reported that a man had exchanged altered bills" at the banks where they worked. Both employees got his license number; it had been issued to a Bert E. Cole. Agents began surveillance at the man's San Francisco address. "On the morning of May 7, 1936, Special Agents assigned to the FBI's San Francisco Field Office were instructed to search that neighborhood. Two Agents found a Ford with the reported license number in a parking lot enclosed by a wire fence." While they kept watch, a man got in the car and tried to start it. When he got out and lifted the hood, the authorities approached him, and he said his name was William Dainard. He was quickly divested of his .45 Colt automatic pistol and $37,374.47 "in money and bills that Dainard admitted he had received in exchange for the ransom money." Eventually, agents were able to recover $14,000 in $100 bills that he had divided, burying some in Utah and hiding some in the garage of his Los Angeles home, plus "various dyes and other paraphernalia used to change serial numbers on paper currency."

Dainard admitted to being part of the kidnapping and was transferred to Tacoma. On May 9, 1936, he entered a guilty plea in the United States District Court. He was sentenced to two concurrent sixty-year prison terms for kidnapping and conspiring to kidnap. Immediately following the trial, he was sent to the McNeil Island Penitentiary and then was transferred to the federal penitentiary at Leavenworth, Kansas. There, prison authorities found him to be insane and recommended that he be confined to a hospital. He spent time at a mental hospital in Springfield, Missouri, before being sent to Alcatraz.

Agents also discovered he had an accomplice, Edward Fliss, who had helped to exchange the ransom money. Fliss was arrested at the Delmar Hotel in San Francisco, offered no resistance and confessed to helping Dainard. At court in Seattle, he pleaded guilty and was sentenced to ten years in prison and a $5,000 fine.

Both Waleys wanted to avoid "Washington's kidnapping law which called for the death penalty unless the jury" opted for lesser charges.

Margaret Waley pleaded not guilty but lost and received two concurrent twenty-year terms in the United States Detention Farm in Milan, Michigan. She served thirteen years and, when released, divorced Harmon. She remarried, moved to Salt Lake and died in 1989 at the age of seventy-four.

Harmon Waley "entered a plea of guilty on June 21, 1935, and was sentenced to serve concurrent prison terms of 45 years" for kidnapping and

2 years on a charge of conspiring to kidnap. He, too, was sent to McNeil Island but then transferred to Alcatraz.

Waley wrote to George Weyerhaeuser from prison several times, apologizing for his actions. Later on, George told KUOW, an NPR radio station, that the man was young, in his twenties at the time of the kidnapping, and didn't mean him any harm. When Waley was paroled on June 3, 1963, at the age of fifty-two, George Weyerhaeuser gave him a job at one of his Oregon plants. Waley died in Salem in 1984 at the age of seventy-three.

Within the personal papers of Dr. Robert G. Green, a bacteriologist in the medical school at the University of Minnesota, is an "FBI wanted persons mailer." The individual named on the mailer is William Dainard, and it "was part of a national attempt to locate Dainard." Dr. Green had received a copy because he was a bacteriologist and it was thought Dainard was likely seeking treatment for a venereal disease. In this case, the FBI used Dainard's social activities and subsequent social disease against him in an effort to track him down. However, Dainard was ninety when he died in 1992 in Great Falls, Montana.

Edward Fliss disappeared into history after serving most of his ten-year term.

Chapter 24

KIDNAPPING NO. 3

Charles Mattson Is Snatched from His Home

It must have seemed as if Tacoma was becoming kidnapping central. First Arthur Rust in 1921, then George Weyerhaeuser in 1935 and, in 1936, Charles Mattson.

On Sunday evening, December 27, 1936, ten-year-old Charles Mattson was taken from his home at 4605 North Verde Street at gunpoint in the presence of his brother Billy, sixteen, and sister Muriel and her friend Virginia Chatfield of Seattle, both fourteen. Dr. and Mrs. Mattson were away from home at a social event, and the children were in the living room eating popcorn and drinking root beer. At approximately 8:45 p.m., someone began pounding on the French doors at the rear of the house that opened onto a terrace. Charles went to see who it was and ran back to the living room, saying he'd seen a masked man standing in front of the glass doors. While the children listened, the man continued pounding, demanding entry and muttering incoherently. They refused to open the door, so he broke some glass panes with the butt of his gun, reached in and turned the latch. Once inside, he menaced the children with his revolver, shouting, "Don't you kids try anything, because I have a bullet-proof vest on." The intruder demanded money and searched Billy's pockets. Finding nothing, he muttered, "A home such as this should be good for some money." While he was talking and while Billy was saying that they did not keep money in the house, the intruder's mask slipped, revealing his face to the children.

Then the intruder gestured to Charlie, saying, "I want you to come with me. You're your father's favorite so you're worth more money." He told

Charles Mattson and his sister. *Courtesy of the Tacoma Public Library.*

the children not to call the police or he'd come back and shoot them, and then he dropped a ransom note in the glass shards on the floor. Grabbing Charles by the arm, he pulled him through the French doors. The remaining children watched as the kidnapper ran across the backyard to a path that "led down a steep, 300-foot, terraced embankment to a picnic ground and swimming pool," from there to the railroad tracks and finally to Ruston Way on the waterfront.

Billy immediately called the police, who quickly arrived, and then called his parents. The children described the kidnapper as thirty-five to forty years old, about five feet, seven inches and of medium weight. He was swarthy and unshaven and had dark hair, brown eyes and a foreign accent. He wore a dark blue jacket, dark work trousers and a brown-and-white checkered cap. Charles, they said, was four feet, six inches and wore a gray sweater, blue knickerbockers and slippers.

After ruling out escape by boat because of an exceptionally low tide, the police thought the kidnapper may have had a car parked on Ruston Way. They immediately began what became an all-night search throughout the area, both in patrol cars and on foot.

A year and a half had passed since the last major kidnapping involving the FBI. Now notified of the abduction, a spokesman for the bureau said the Federal Kidnapping Act had likely been violated; nine agents were immediately sent to Tacoma to assist the police. Within a week, another thirty-one arrived, and the kidnapper was declared Public Enemy No. 1. Assistant director Harold Nathan and inspector Earl J. Connelly, who had successfully directed the Weyerhaeuser case eighteen months earlier, arrived from the bureau to take charge.

The ransom note left at the Mattson home was folded and pocket-worn, looking as if it had been made on a child's toy typewriter using an odd color ink. At first, officers took it to be rambling and incoherent, but a closer analysis showed the note to be poorly spelled but succinct. "The price is 28,000 10000 in fives and 10s 18000 50 & 100s," it read, and "Old bills pleasd [*sic*] no new ones. Put ad in *Seattle Times* personal colum [*sic*] read 'Mable—What's your new address Tim.' Put this ad *Times* no other paper. If no answer from you within week price gos [*sic*] up double and doubl [*sic*] that each week after. Dont [*sic*] fail & I won't [*sic*]. The boy is safe. Tim"

Two days after the kidnapping, someone did put an ad in the classified section of the Seattle paper that read, "Mable—Please give us your address. Ann." The Mattsons denied knowledge of the ad, but a special delivery letter arrived at their home, causing a "flurry of obvious excitement among the tensely waiting family." The letter said anyone could deliver the ransom as long as the person drove a Ford and was alone. It also said, "Ignore all messages delivered to you unless they are written in the same letters and the same color ink as this. Tim"

Within minutes of the letter's arrival, chief jailor and former King County sheriff Matt Starwich and Undersheriff Louis Forbes arrived at the home. They had a short conversation with Muriel and left as quickly as they had come. It was thought that they might be considering using the services of Tacoma's famous "dog detective, Ing," a police bloodhound who'd had uncanny success in tracking down criminals in the past. However, there is no mention of his ever being used.

Orders went out to arrest a musician named Tim who had suddenly disappeared from his regular haunts. Suspicion also centered on another musician and known narcotic addict. Public interest then centered on a forty-minute visit made to Dr. Mattson by Lieutenant Colonel Gus B. Appelman, believed to be the go-between for the family and the kidnapper. Along with everyone else at the home was John S. Strickland, a retired police captain and family friend.

As the story continued to be front-page news, all kinds of things were printed: his mother's concerns because Charles had just recovered from a cold and wouldn't be warm enough; his grandmother's fear that the boy would suffer being away from his mother, to whom he was very close. She offered to be the intermediary and to give the kidnapper all the property she and her husband owned. Phone lines when no officers were on guard and uninterrupted mail service were made available. Paul H. Sceva, another family friend, thought at least two men were involved. He thought the kidnappers had gotten away by boat, and police canvassed the waterfront again.

On January 11, 1937, nineteen-year-old Gordon Morrow "was hunting rabbits on a snow-covered field of brush and stumps, behind his home in Snohomish County, approximately four-and-a-half miles south of Everett, when he stumbled across the naked body of a young boy, lying frozen in the fresh snow in a thicket of alder saplings. His wrists were tied, and he had been stabbed in the back and beaten severely." He appeared to have massive head injuries. Gordon ran home and told his father, Charles Morrow, and they returned to the site to look at the body, after which Gordon ran a half mile through the snow to a nearby gasoline service station and telephoned Snohomish County sheriff Walter E. Faulkner with the news of his discovery.

At the site, "150 feet west of the Edmonds–Beverly Park Road and approximately one-half mile west of Pacific Highway, sheriff's deputies discovered tire tracks and footprints in the snow" and felt the boy had been murdered elsewhere and left there late Sunday night or early Monday morning. Gordon Morrow thought the body was probably left about 9:00

p.m. on Sunday when his bulldog, Nick, started barking excitedly and running from door to door, trying to get out of the house.

For fifteen days, the hunt for Charles's kidnapper made national news. FBI director J. Edgar Hoover said, "We will use all the resources at our command to apprehend and bring to justice the kidnapper and slayer of the Mattson boy." President Franklin D. Roosevelt offered a $10,000 reward for "information leading to the arrest of a suspect" and promised that the case would be pursued until the killer was arrested, and far and wide, suspects were being interviewed.

By the end of 1938, sixteen thousand men, including all viable prisoners sent to various penitentiaries, had been questioned. Eventually, that number grew by ten thousand more. Despite the best efforts of the nation, the kidnapper was never caught and the case never solved.

Dr. William Mattson died on November 23, 1968. Hazel Velma Fletcher Mattson died on August 7, 1978. They and their son are buried at Tacoma Mausoleum.

Eric Russell, son of George Russell, founder of the Russell Investment Group, bought the Mattsons' Tudor-style home in 2006 and had it torn down.

Though investigative efforts ceased decades ago, the Mattson case continues to be described as the oldest unsolved kidnapping on the federal books.

Part V

....

LEAVING THE DEPRESSION BEHIND

Chapter 25

GALLOPING GERTIE
AND THE PREMIUMS THIEF

As far back as 1889, both sides of the Narrows Straits were angling for a bridge to connect Tacoma and the Kitsap Peninsula. In 1888 or 1889, rancher John G. Shindler went through the strait on a steamboat, pointed to the bluffs and said to the ship captain, "Someday you will see a bridge over these narrows." A clerk in the Northern Pacific Railroad's land office also saw the merits of the idea and proposed a link from Tacoma to Port Orchard, where the Puget Sound Naval Shipyard was based. However, it was felt there was no economic reason to justify the connection, and the idea faded.

It's true that in 1914, Aaron Titlow had a ferry in conjunction with his Titlow Resort, but it mainly traveled to Henderson Bay and back. According to harborhistorymyseum.blogspot.com, on June 8, 1928, though, "ferry traffic began between Point Fosdick and the end of Sixth Avenue in Tacoma."

In 1923, neighborhood improvement clubs on the city's north end became the first serious promoters of an across-the-straits connection, and the Federated Improvement Clubs of Tacoma proposed a bridge between Point Defiance and Gig Harbor. The club president told reporters that they had been working on the project for several months. Their efforts came to naught. Three years later, the Tacoma Chamber of Commerce "endorsed a campaign for a bridge across the Narrows." However, the county had given a ten-year contract to Mitchell Skansie for a ferry service, and his contract included a no-competition clause. Nevertheless, the chamber of commerce hired E.M. Chandler, an Olympia man, to build a bridge. He suggested a suspension bridge costing $3 million and requested a loan "from the government's newly-created Reconstruction Finance Corporation," with tolls to repay the loan. The RFC refused, citing too little traffic plus the cost to buy out the Skansie ferry system. A month later, Chandler had a new plan, but it had little support. A year passed before the Departments of the Army and Navy saw the value of a link between Fort Lewis and the Bremerton Shipyards. The county applied to the Public Works Agency for funds, but initially, the bureaucracy seemed to sit on the idea. Not until 1936, when the War Department approved a revised application for a $4 million suspension bridge, did it provide a grant for 45 percent of the cost. County public utility bonds would cover the rest.

The original Tacoma Narrows Bridge was the first bridge of which Latvia-born Leon Moisseiff, a prominent suspension bridge engineer, was the leading engineer. He called the design the "most beautiful bridge in the world." Agents in Washington's Highway Department called it "fundamentally unsound" because "it was lighter and narrower than any bridge ever built." Nevertheless, bids went out, and construction began on November 23, 1938. The grand opening was July 1, 1940.

Pretty much from the beginning, the Narrows Bridge moved. Suspension bridges are supposed to move, but this was different. Sometimes the span bounced for a few minutes, sometimes for up to six to eight hours; sometimes it rippled, sometimes it had two- to three-foot "waves." Motorists became seasick, but thrill-seekers loved it.

Then, at 11:00 a.m. on November 7, 1940, four months after it opened, an "aero-elastic flutter" triggered by a forty-two-mile-per-hour wind caused the bridge to collapse. During the bridge's four-month existence, assuming the facilities at Point Fosdick would no longer be needed, their dismantling had begun. Now, with Galloping Gertie's collapse, Washington Navigation Company, which ran the ferries, had to scramble. Ferry owner Skansie told his wife, "We're back in business again!" Ferries began to run the next morning, November 8.

While the Point Fosdick landing was proving unusable, in Tacoma the blame game began. Clark Eldridge, a project engineer, said, "The men who held the purse-strings were the whip-crackers on the entire project. We had a tried-and-true conventional bridge design. We were told we couldn't have the necessary money without using plans furnished by an eastern firm of engineers chosen by the money-lenders." He and other state engineers had protested Moisseiff's design with its eight-foot solid girders, which he called "sails," to no avail.

THIS TIME THE ANGULAR DISTORTION

An undulating bridge. *Courtesy of the Library of Congress.*

Public Works Administration officials said they knew nothing about a problem with the bridge's design. On July 11, 1941, the *Tacoma Times* reported that the PWA's field engineer, David L. Glenn, had "submitted a report warning of faults in design and refusing to recommend acceptance of the structure. But, the PWA accepted the bridge. So did the Washington State Toll Bridge Authority." Two weeks after the story made headlines, Glenn was "relieved of his position."

Insurance companies filed a report on June 2, 1941, saying "they believed the piers, cables, and towers could be salvaged and reused." They offered the state a settlement of $1.8 million. Three weeks later, the state submitted its own claim. Saying the bridge was a virtual loss, it asked for "almost $4.3 million." The two sides reached an agreement of $4 million in August 1941.

Unfortunately, while negotiations were going on, it was discovered that though Hallett R. French, an agent for Merchants' Fire Assurance Company of New York, had written an $800,000 policy on the bridge, he felt there was no chance that the bridge would collapse. Consequently, he deposited the $8,000 in premiums in his own account. Word of the collapse ruined his Idaho vacation. On December 2, 1940, Seattle police arrested him on charges of grand larceny. Bail was denied. "French returned approximately $17,500 in missing funds which included the Narrows premiums and monies from unrelated policies." Though his friends pleaded for leniency, French pleaded guilty and was sentenced to fifteen years to be served at the Walla Walla State Penitentiary. He was paroled after two years and went to work in one of Seattle's shipyards. He died in 1968.

Chapter 26

THE HORROR THAT
WAS JAKE BIRD

Five myths persist regarding serial killers: they are all men (17 percent are female); they are mainly Caucasian; they are isolated and dysfunctional loners; they travel widely and kill interstate; they are either mentally ill or evil geniuses. Serial killer Jake Bird fits three of the myths. He was male, he did travel widely and he did kill interstate, but he was a competent Black man who was not a dysfunctional loner.

Bird was one of three boys born to Charles and Delie Bird somewhere in Louisiana; he never knew exactly where. He and brothers Andrew and Lem grew up very poor, and in 1920, at age nineteen, he left home and began traveling the country, sneaking into train cars in one town and hopping off in another. Like most hobos, he traded a day's work for a night's sleep and a warm meal wherever he could, repeating the process over and over. Sometimes, he was a manual laborer; other times, he was a railroad gandy dancer, laying and maintaining tracks, with the railroad moving him from place to place—Ohio (he said he beat a man and woman to death in Cleveland with a brick and partially dismembered them and disposed of the bodies in the Bull Run area), California (he confessed to killing a grocer in Los Angeles), Illinois (where he slit the throat of a man in Chicago and killed a woman while trying to grab her purse; both bodies were dumped in Lake Michigan), New York (he shot a delicatessen operator in Hell's Kitchen), Iowa, Kansas, Kentucky, Nebraska, South Dakota, Wisconsin, Florida, Illinois and, finally, Tacoma, Washington. His killing spree began in 1930 and included stalking, robbing, raping, mutilating and murdering his victims.

Newspaper articles about Bird begin in July 1928, when he complained to railroad officials in Omaha of having been beaten with a sap by one of their guards. Articles about the incident—during which one of Bird's fellow boxcar riders was also beaten up and eventually died—ran for four months in newspapers throughout the Midwest. Then, on November 23, Mrs. Harold Stribling positively identified him as Omaha's "hatchet slayer."

She and her husband had been attacked in their home, their attacker crushing Mr. Stribling's head with a hatchet. While she was in a hospital bed, the police had shown the injured woman multiple photographs of likely perpetrators, but when they ushered Bird into her room, she said, "That's the man," and became hysterical. Bird was immediately taken to the state penitentiary, and the *Bismarck Daily Tribune* weighed in, saying he was a former convict who had done time in Utah for burglary and rape. The *Chicago Daily News* said Mrs. Stribling was Bird's fifth victim. The attack on the Striblings followed three killings in three days. J.W. Blackman was bludgeoned to death, and Gertrude Resso and her sister Creda Brown were killed while asleep. The police were never able to make a case against Bird for these crimes or for a fourth person who was badly wounded or fifth who sustained less dire injuries. Bird said he was innocent of the Stribling attacks, and a waitress said he was in her restaurant while the attack took place. However, Mrs. Stribling stood by her identification, and while the police tried to match fingerprints, they learned that Bird, under the names J.C. Bird or Jake Byrd, had a lengthy record on the Pacific coast: arrested in 1922 for impersonating an officer; arrested on November 21, 1922, in Oakland, California, for larceny; arrested twice in 1924 in Salt Lake City on burglary charges and released on July 6, 1926, by Los Angeles authorities after a hearing on a robbery charge. Then, a second lady, a Mrs. Hankins, came forth and identified Bird as a man who tried to force his way into her house. "That was the way he stood in front of me," she said. "I never can forget his eyes, his lips, his coat and cap, even his shoes. He's wearing the same shoes today he wore the morning I saw him."

"Lady, I don't know what you're talking about," Bird said.

While a representative for the NAACP said he felt Bird was innocent, the suspect was taken to the Iowa State Penitentiary at Fort Madison to await trial. Meanwhile, the police were working on fingerprint evidence. Bird was indicted and asked for a change of venue. His defenders sold buttons, with the proceeds going to help with his legal fees. When the trial began on February 1, 1929, excitement ran so high that people were bartering their courtroom seats. After he was found guilty, Bird said, "Well, it's a tough break." He was sentenced to thirty years.

Following his early release, Bird's freedom didn't last long. In April 1943, he was in a Michigan jail, having committed a series of burglaries "in a fashionable part of town." The papers didn't say how long Bird's Michigan sentence was, but he faded from the newspaper scene until October 30, 1947, when he was arrested in Tacoma for the axe murders of fifty-three-year-old Bertha Kludt, a baker at a local department store, and her seventeen-year-old daughter Beverly June Kludt, a recent high school graduate.

Police officers A.B. Sabutis and Evan Davies were called to the house when neighbors heard screams. As they approached, a man burst out the back door, passed Sabutis and headed toward Davies, who gave chase. The officers cornered him in a clump of bushes. During a fight to subdue him, both officers were cut by a large spike the man carried, Davies on his hands and Sabutis on the back, and both Sabutis and the assailant would require hospitalization.

Once the man was under control, the officers entered the house and found the bodies of the two women. Both of them had been struck on the backs of their heads, bludgeoned and hacked. The man the officers arrested identified himself as Jake Bird. He confessed, saying he'd taken an axe into the house through an unlatched back door "to bluff anyone who tried to bother me." Mrs. Kludt's bedroom was off the kitchen, and Detective Lieutenant Earl Cornelison later said Bird had attempted to rape her. Her screams brought her daughter to the room, and as they fought him, he killed them both with the axe. Mrs. Kludt was found beside her bed and her daughter in the blood-spattered kitchen. Bird was booked for investigation but held without charge.

After Bird's arrest, three things happened: Officer John Hickey beat him up; newspaper photographer Frank Herbert took pictures of Bird in his isolation cell, saying, "Through the bars he saw a six-foot-tall bald black man of about 185 pounds who had a hole in the top of his nose, swollen skin around his eyes, and puffed-up cheeks. His clothes were spattered with dry blood stains [and] he lay like a dissected frog on the iron bed"; and forensics pathologist Dr. Charles Larson "high-tailed it from the murder scene to County Hospital where Bird was being held in the prison ward and asked for his clothing."

Larson's credentials were impeccable. Among other things, he was a founding member of the American Academy of Forensic Sciences and a member of the National Association of Medical Examiners. He was certified in pathologic anatomy, clinical pathology and forensic pathology by the American Board of Pathology and the American Board of Legal Medicine. Years after World War II ended, he was still reluctant to talk about what he'd seen and the work he did at German concentration camps.

Called to the Kludt crime scene, he saw that Mrs. Kludt had been hit on the head so hard that her skull had been fractured and the sack of membrane that encloses the brain in a cushion of liquid had been ruptured. He found brain tissue in her hair and on the floor. Bird's clothing had blood smears and brain tissue on his cuffs. This was good news for prosecuting attorney Pat Steele, who felt, despite the confession, that he had a weak case. None of the evidence had been properly identified or marked.

Larson also interviewed the prisoner, later saying Bird had read a lot about the law while in prisons and that he was "sharp as a tack, an avid reader, an able conversationalist, and witty." He added, "He was a very sophisticated burglar. He could talk you right out of your socks." But he also said that Bird was calculating, hated white people and "that he'd snuff out a human life the way you'd smash a fly."

Others called him "dangerous as sin but fascinating."

Bird said since he had left Louisiana in 1920, he'd had no home. Eleven days before the Kludt murders, he quit an "extra gang" in Pocatello, Idaho, and visited Spokane and Seattle before arriving in Tacoma. He said he'd confessed to ease his conscience, a confession he later changed.

When what amounted to a three-day trial started on November 23, 1947, Larson made it a point to address his responses to the jury. His testimony left the defense with little argument. The jury took thirty-five minutes to find Bird guilty. During sentencing, Bird said the police had forced the confession out of him. While he was complaining about police treatment, a woman at the back of the room jumped up, screaming, "Let that man go! He is not guilty! He is innocent!" She was removed, and the judge sentenced Bird to be hanged at the Washington State Penitentiary on January 16, 1948.

Bird then put a hex on "all of you who had anything to do with my being punished," saying, "Mark my words; you will die before I do."

Was his hex responsible for the deaths of five people connected with the trial?

<u>Edward D. Hodge</u>, Pierce County Superior Court judge, age sixty-nine, had a heart attack and died on January 1, 1948, within a month of sentencing.

<u>Joseph E. Karpach,</u> Pierce County undersheriff, age forty-six, died April 5, 1948.

<u>George L. Harrigan,</u> Pierce County court reporter, age sixty-nine, died June 11, 1948.

<u>Sherman W. Lyons</u>, Tacoma police detective lieutenant, age forty-six, died October 28, 1948.

<u>James W. Selden,</u> Bird's defense attorney, age seventy-six, died on November 26, 1948, the first anniversary of Bird's sentencing.

When Bird "claimed he had committed 44 other murders which he was willing to help the police solve," Washington governor Monrad C. Wallgren granted him a sixty-day reprieve. Police from other states interviewed Bird, and eleven murders were substantiated. He was also knowledgeable enough about the thirty-three other murders to be considered a prime suspect. During his reprieve, Bird lodged an appeal, but the Washington State Supreme Court denied him a retrial. His appeals to the federal courts, including three petitions to the United States Supreme Court, were also denied.

The Reverend C. Arvid Orhnell heard Bird's confession, and it was to him that Bird confessed to fourteen murders. He also read Bird's brief statement, which said he "bore malice toward no one; that he no longer had hatred in [his] heart."

Bird was executed at the Walla Walla Penitentiary on June 15, 1949, at 12:30 a.m. He hung for fourteen minutes before being declared dead. No one claimed the body, and he was buried at the prison cemetery under his prison number, 21520.

A crowd of 120 people witnessed his hanging. Some were victims' family members; others were police officials from the Midwest and Pacific Northwest.

Bird left a twenty-page handwritten memoir, partially released by his attorney. It led to authorities solving at least eleven murders, mostly in the Midwest.

Jake Bird cost Washington State $4,575.00 and Pierce County $2,811.06, plus an additional $3,000.00 for various guards, officers and officials. The most expensive "item" was the cost of transporting "the noose-skipping-bird" to and from Pierce County four times to have death warrants signed.

In February 1959, Harold Stribling shot his wife and killed himself.

In January 1964, Washington State decided to divest itself of the "infamous criminal guns" and other weapons in its possession that had been used in a variety of crimes. Some had disappeared; some were auctioned off; others were returned to the counties from where they had come. County officials were supposed to return them to the original owners or to the various defense attorneys or prosecuting attorneys involved in the crimes. According to the *Oregonian*, Jake Bird's double-bladed axe had disappeared.

Chapter 27

BAD BOYS OF WORLD WAR II

*O*n December 8, 1941, the day after the Pearl Harbor attack, state and federal officials started working to get the country on war footing. People in Europe, of course, had been preparing since 1939. During a blackout, to protect his moustache—which measured seventeen inches from tip to tip—Harry Williams of Margate, England, tied the ends together with white tape. Now, in the United States, blackouts were part of the new norm going forward.

For many people, the imposed blackouts, conducted on a regular basis, were a nuisance. For Tacoma's Selden Furniture and Carpet Company, they were a business saver. Initially, and to comply with the regulations, people painted their windows black or covered them at night with blankets—both inconvenient and, in warm weather, very uncomfortable. Selden was one of many firms that "started producing and selling blackout blinds for commercial and home use." In 1942, the Selden plant went on a sixteen-hour, six-days-a-week production schedule to meet demand. On one occasion, it had more than thirty thousand orders. In addition to non-military blackout blinds, defense housing projects also required thousands of blinds. They, plus sales of linoleum and carpets, saved the company.

All over the country, streetlights were dimmed, covered with shields to throw the glow downward or turned off altogether. Traffic lights and vehicle headlights were fitted with slotted covers to direct the beam down toward the ground. The result was that thousands of people died in road accidents.

People were encouraged to walk facing traffic, and it was suggested that men on foot leave their white shirttails hanging out. Robberies, rapes and even murders were common occurrences. Gang-related activities, frauds and cons were rampant. People tripped, fell down stairs and bumped into things. In Tacoma, five people were "gassed by fumes from a smudge pot used to mark an 'incident' during a half-hour test blackout and incident drill." In Seattle, a man named Matt Starwich fell off a ledge of the County-City Building; at the north end of the Allentown Bridge, a man in a 1941 model coupe missed the bridge and drove into the Duwamish River. It was just good luck that city officials in Tacoma were able to find $250 for the construction of hoods for Stadium Bowl's high-powered lights so nighttime football could continue.

Army officers recommended driving no faster than twenty miles an hour during blackout periods. Drivers caught when sirens went off had to immediately pull over, leave their cars unlocked and head for the nearest shelter. Fishermen were barred from access to Puget Sound before sunrise and after sunset, and duck hunters in boats needed Coast Guard permits. No cameras were allowed on boats in Tacoma, Olympia, Seattle or Everett waters.

If necessary, Tacoma could call on the Coast Guard, National Guard and Fort Lewis's bomb disposal units for help. However, though a possible coastal invasion was a very real fear, blackouts weren't always well received. Lights leaked out from jukeboxes and pinball machines. Noncompliant business merchants claimed to have misplaced their blackout curtains. In Seattle, a woman incited a riot because lights were coming out of store windows, specifically the Foreman and Clark store. When the *News Tribune* reported that an "eastern scatterbrain" was running around town with a flashlight and was arrested and given fifteen days "in the cooler," one wit said, "The charge was battery."

Tacoma had 5,500 Civil Defense volunteers who were sometimes thought to be overzealous. At 9325 South Tacoma Way, L.A. Spargo, operator of El Rancho Motor Court, was arrested for refusing to turn off his "No Vacancy" sign. Although both the local and district wardens had approved the sign, an obsessive patrol officer found Spargo in violation of the blackout regulations. The case went to trial in Justice Clarence E. Layton's court, and the sign was found to cast no more light than a gas pump. The charges were thrown out.

However, in 1943, the Tacoma Sportsmen's Club, then located at 903 Commerce Street, didn't get off so easy. Information the War Production Board turned over to the Department of Justice resulted in the entire elected board, all directors, the club manager and the contractor—eleven men in

A warning from the government.
Courtesy of the Library of Congress.

all—being charged with violating the second war powers act. On February 18, their bail was set at $500 each, and the club itself was fined $5,000. The charge was that the men knowingly diverted critical metals and materials—i.e. copper wiring, various pieces of equipment and lumber—and used them to construct and remodel a bar and cocktail room.

Reuben Carlson, the club's attorney, said, "The association was a non-profit and receipts from liquor sales and other activities were used to purchase their building and to promote sports activities in the community."

"I believe justice can be served by the imposition of a fine on the corporation," John Burrell, attorney for the War Department, told the judge, "but the government has insufficient evidence to convict some of the directors and [that] others of the directors may not have been aware that the regulations were being violated." He added that corporate liability, however, "could be established without a doubt."

"I'd be hesitant in assessing such a fine if this case stood alone," the judge said. "It is the effect on the general public by the setting of this example that must be considered. Conviction of the individuals would stamp them as unpatriotic for the rest of their lives. However, ignorance of the law is no excuse." And no charges were brought against the men.

But when it comes to bad behavior, the Tacoma Sportsmen's Club violation runs second to that of Robert Cecil Van Valkenberg.

On December 16, 1943, someone tipped off police officer Eugene Adair that an army deserter was hiding in a house at 6223 South Mason, a home belonging to Robert Cecil and Betty Van Valkenberg. Adair and other officers were familiar with the home. Acting previously on tips from neighbors, they'd made many trips there, and Mrs. Van Valkenberg always said the man her neighbors had seen was just a handyman. However, both the Tacoma and the military police had obligations to check, and on that particular December evening, they acted promptly, reaching the home at 7:15 p.m. Mrs. Van Valkenberg met them at the door and said her husband hadn't been home for two months. Nevertheless, the authorities made an extensive though unsuccessful search. They were about to leave when one of them heard a noise under the floor. Lifting a rug, they saw a trapdoor that, when opened, revealed a stairway leading to a dug-out cellar under the center of the house. The cellar, they soon discovered, was furnished with a cheerfully burning stove, a radio, a workbench with assorted tools and a homemade table on which sat "the still warm remnants of a meal." The only problem was, if someone had made the noise, where was that person? There was no exit other than the stairway.

Since there was no second way out, the officers began probing the walls, but all they found were solid banks of dirt. Something made the noise though—but what? Then one of the investigators discovered that the lower section of the stairway was detachable. The men removed it and uncovered a wooden panel that, with a little maneuvering, slid back. Behind the panel was a six-foot shaft leading to a sub-cellar containing a full-size bed, a chair, books and, on that night, Robert Cecil Van Valkenberg.

Both Robert and Betty were arrested, and though neither had anything to say while together, they both readily talked when separated. Robert told the officers that he was thirty-one, had enlisted in 1935 and was in the Third Division. But by 1941, he wasn't feeling well and had been trying to get a medical discharge. Hearing of Japan's attack on Pearl Harbor, he knew that wouldn't happen, so he decided to go AWOL. While his fellow company members were fighting in Italy and North Africa, he began excavating under his house, doing most of the work at night and taking time off, occasionally, to go trapping in Idaho. He had been in hiding for almost two years.

Betty said the family had been living on Pierce County Welfare Assistance, but she couldn't explain the "apparently expensive and fairly new fur coat she was wearing." Nor would she say how she and her husband had been able to pay for a twenty-five-dollar war bond and forty dollars' worth of war savings stamps.

The pair had two children: Merlyn, age eleven, and nine-month-old Freddy. The day after their parents' arrests—Robert Cecil for desertion and Betty for harboring a fugitive—the children, who were both suffering from unspecified illnesses, were taken to Pierce County Hospital.

Not long after his arrest, Robert was taken back to his Mason Street home to pose for pictures.

CLOSING

$\mathscr{A}$fter an "investigation by a state legislative committee revealed widespread corruption in Tacoma's government," after the "American Social Hygiene Association had given Tacoma a bad rating," after "the Army threatened to put the town off limits to soldiers" and after "accusations had been made that the police were taking payoffs to protect vice operations," clearly, something had to be done. In November 1951, Senator Albert Rosellini began holding "public hearings in the Tacoma Armory as part of a statewide investigation into crime and vice."

The most important testimonies came from four sources; first was the Reverend Loyal J. Vickers, who said that while in Chicago he was approached by two men who said "the Council of Churches would be given $50,000 if he would support a certain (unnamed) candidate." They also said Tacoma was considered "one of the most lucrative places for vice in the United States" and that "Vito Cuttone had asked them to make the offer."

Next was Alma W. Jackson, a relative of Amanda Truelove, who was dubbed by the press as the "Whispering Voice of the Tacoma Crime Hearings." Jackson, who admitted to having been arrested twenty times and still had four cases pending, said she'd paid $825 per month back to 1948 "to enable her to run a house of prostitution." She also said she'd made "bribe payments of $1,600 after numerous raids by police."

When Vito Cuttone testified, he said he was the owner and operator of the Cameo Theater and the owner of real estate in Tacoma and Seattle. He said between 1940 and 1944, he'd owned 149 pinball machines, but he sold them, explaining that he "got tired of it [the business]."

Then it was Amanda Truelove's turn, and she "dropped a bombshell." Among talk of payoffs, she said, "In August 1951 James T. Kerr, Commissioner of Public Safety and then Police Chief Anthony 'Tony' Zatkovich asked her to sign a statement that she had not paid protection money to anyone in the police department or anyone else since Kerr took office in June 1950"—something both men categorically denied.

Unfortunately, the proceedings seemed to have accomplished nothing. After six days of televised hearings, Tacoma continued to be called a "Vice Capital," "Sin City" or "Seattle's Dirty Backyard."

Vito Cuttone died on February 10, 1958, and is buried at Calvary Cemetery in Tacoma. He was sixty-five.

Amanda Truelove Buckley was seventy-seven when she died in May 1966. Tuell Funeral Homes handled her services, but her obituary doesn't say where she was buried.

Alma Jackson was in and out of trouble until 1957. She died on March 17, 1970.

When Cuttone was in a car accident, Frank Magrini "allegedly took over the rackets in Tacoma." He died on September 17, 1965.

Racketeering, however, was not going away. On December 8, 1978, a federal grand jury indicted fifteen men in Pierce County "for engaging in a widespread racketeering conspiracy." The gang, known as "The Enterprise," led by Tacoma mobster John Joseph Carbone, was "charged with using assault, arson, extortion, bribery, and attempted murder in an effort to control Pierce County's topless-dancing tavern business." The Enterprise was also said to have "actively engaged in insurance fraud, protection, prostitution, and illegal gambling." When it was finally taken down, six men pleaded guilty, and seven more were found guilty at trial. Only one, David Willard Levage, was found not guilty. But then, he was already serving twenty years in state prison for setting fire to the Top of the Ocean restaurant.

BIBLIOGRAPHY

Websites

CPI Inflation Calculator. www.bls.gov/data/inflation_calculator.htm.
Digital Scholarship at UNLV. digitalscholarship.unlv.edu.
Eyewitness to History. EyewitnesstoHistory.com.
Find a Grave. Findagrave.com.
Genealogy Bank. genealogybank.com.
The Hall of Valor Project. valor.militarytimes.com.
Harbor History Museum Blog. harborhistorymuseum.blogspot.com.
History Link. historylink.org.
Humane Society. humanesociety.org.
Lewiston Tribune. lmtribune.com/northwest.
North Star Monthly. northstarmonthly.com.
Rivertowns. rivertowns.net.
Small, Andrew. "The Wastelands of Urban Renewal." Bloomberg, February 13, 2017. citylab.com/equity/2017/02/urban-renewal-wastelands/516378.
South Sound Business. southsoundbiz.com/examiner.
Tacoma History. tacomahistory.live.
Tacoma Prohibition Tales. tacomaprohibitiontales.wordpress.com.
Today I Found Out. todayifoundout.com.
University of Minnesota Libraries. archives.lib.umn.edu.
Washington State. wsm.wsu.edu.

BIBLIOGRAPHY

Wikipedia. Wikipedia.org.
Yakima Herald. yakimaherald.com.

Articles

Hayes, Robert. "Shanghaied." In *Landsman Hay: The Memoirs of Robert Hay, 1789–1847*. Edited by M.D. Hay. N.p.: Rupert Hart-Davis, 1811.

Books

Huggins, Edward. *Journal of Occurrences at Muck Station Puget Sound Agricultural Company, 1858–1859: A Farm of the Puget's Sound Agricultural company [sic] in Pierce County, Washington Territory*. Tacoma, WA: Tacoma Public Library, 1984.

Hunt, Herbert. *Tacoma, Its History and Its Builders: A Half Century of Activity*. 3 vols. Chicago: S.J. Clarke Publishing Company, 1915.

McCallum, John D. *Crime Doctor*. Vancouver, Canada: Gordon Soules Book Publishers, 1978.

Ott, John S., and Dick Malloy. *The Tacoma Public Utilities Story: The First 100 Years*. Tacoma, WA: Tacoma Public Utilities, 1993.

Prosch, Charles. *Reminiscences of Washington Territory: Scenes, Incidents and Reflections of the Pioneer Period on Puget Sound*. Seattle, WA, 1904.

Stover, Karla. *Hidden History of Tacoma: Little-Known Tales from the City of Destiny*. Charleston, SC: The History Press, 2012.

———. *Tacoma Curiosities: Geoduck Derbies, the Whistling Well of the North End, Alligators in Snake Lake & More*. Charleston, SC: The History Press, 2016.

Timothy, Eric. *More Than a Century of Service: The History of the Tacoma Police Department*. Privately published.

Newspapers

Journal
The News Tribune
Salt Lake Telegram
Seattle Daily Times
Seattle Post-Intelligencer

BIBLIOGRAPHY

Seattle Star
Senior Scene Tacoma
Tacoma Commerce
Tacoma Daily Ledger
Tacoma Daily News
Tacoma Times
Tacoma Weekly Globe
Washington Standard
Weekly Ledger
Weekly Pacific Tribune

ABOUT THE AUTHOR

Karla Stover was born and raised in Tacoma, Washington, and graduated from the University of Washington with honors in history. She has been writing for more than twenty-five years. Her credits include the *News Tribune*, the *Tacoma Reporter*, the *Tacoma Weekly*, *Country Pleasures* magazine and the *Puget Sound Business Journal*. Nationally, she has published in *Ruralite* and *Birds and Blooms*. Internationally, she was a regular contributor to the *European Crown* and the *Imperial Russian Journal*. In 2008, she won the Chistell Prize for a short story titled "One Day at Appomattox." For over fifteen years, she hosted a radio program discussing Tacoma and local history on KLAY AM 1180. Her book *Let's Go Walk About in Tacoma* came out in August 2009. Since then, she has published *Hidden History of Tacoma: Little-Known Tales from the City of Destiny*; *Tacoma Curiosities: Geoduck Derbies, the Whistling Well of the North End, Alligators in Snake Lake and More*; *A Line to Murder*; *Murder: When One Isn't Enough*; *A Feather for a Fan*; and *Wynter's Way*. She is currently working on a novel based on the lives of the Everleigh sisters.

Visit us at
www.historypress.com